how my son learned to speak

a child's discovery of language

written by Isaac Evans
written down by Lloyd Evans

numismabooks.co.uk

'When your foot really hurted you should had a bandage'
Isaac, four years, two months

Foreword

This book happened by accident. When I was 43, my wife and I had a son, Isaac – our only child.

I'm a journalist and I spend a lot of time at home so I was able to monitor Isaac's early development. One day, when he was 21 months old, he suddenly said 'door.' His first word. This seemed so amazing that I began to write down everything he said in a computer file, *Quotable Isaac.*

My initial instinct, as a reporter, was to make money from Isaac's verbal efforts by writing a piece about him. Which I did.

The article is reprinted here. The rest of the book comes from *Quotable Isaac.*

You may want to post a review of this book on Amazon. Each review encourages the algorithm to lift the book's position in the rankings. Earning money interests me less than gaining new readers. That's why I set the price at the minimum allowed by KDP.

How My Son Learned to Speak

numismabooks.co.uk

ISBN 978-1-8384784-2-1

Print edition ISBN 978-1-8384784-3-8

CONTENTS

Age One....1
Age Two....4
Age Three....28
Age Four....56
Age Five....86
Age Six....127
Age Seven....174
Age Eight....202
Gap of two years lost!....217
Age Ten....219
Age Eleven....220
Age Twelve....228
Age Thirteen....237
Age Fourteen....243
Age Fifteen....247
Age Sixteen....248
About the author....249

Age **One**

A Child's First Words

[reprinted courtesy of the *Guardian*]

Isaac was 21 months old, and bumbling around the house, when he suddenly pointed at the sitting-room door.

'Door!'

He aimed a digit towards the painted panels. Door! His first word. I'd been teaching him English for ages, without result. Now, a breakthrough. My pupil had spoken. I gave him a cuddle and made a big fuss of him and got him to repeat 'door.' Which he did. Then I started on his second word.

'Window.'

It was obvious. A window is like a door. An oblong aperture, common in houses, that seals or unseals a gap in a wall. I assumed that Isaac would see the resemblance and say 'window' within a few minutes. Or later that day.

'Window, Isaac.'

Nothing. I tried and tried – but I didn't realise that 'window' is a far harder challenge for the muscles of the tongue and the mouth. To say 'door' you just utter a consonant, 'duh', followed by a noise, or a vowel, 'uuuh.' But 'window' is twice as long and it features two consonants rammed together, 'nd', which is difficult to vocalise. It baffles many foreigners including Spaniards, Finns and Japanese who insert a third vowel between the 'n' and the 'd.' *Window* is beyond them. They say *winner dough.*

I kept my hopes up. As he toddled around the place I pointed to windows in the bathroom and the kitchen. 'Window, Isaac?' We visited every room in the house.

'Window! Window Isaac?'

As we climbed onto my bike to go shopping, I pointed to our bay windows.

'Isaac? Window.'

We sailed along the street to the child-minder's and I kept pointing.

'A window, Isaac. Another window. Isaac? Look. Window?'

I couldn't understand it. Then came his second word 'bike' which he vocalised as 'buy.' He knew the 'k' was there but it was beyond him to include it. And 'buy' was enough.

'Buy' he said pointing to my bike. He got a big reward. Lots of cuddles and laughs and squeals of approval.

'Buy! Yes. It's a buy.'

That's when I twigged how hard 'window' would be. Next he said 'tree' but the 'tr' was too much and he settled for 'tee.' Now he knew three words. And at this point he made a momentous decision. He was fluent in English. He'd mastered the course and was now in a position to teach others, namely me. His rule was that every English noun begins with 't' (apart from bike and door). So 'key' is 'tee' and 'cow' is 'tao' (rhyming with 'how'). 'Car' is 'tar.' Ball is 'taw' and so on. He got very dogmatic about this and he corrected my blunders when we visited the city farm near Canary Wharf.

'Tao,' he said, pointing at a cow.
'No, Isaac,' I suggested gently, 'you mean cow.'
'Tao,' he said, dismissing my mistake.

'Sorry, Isaac,' I repeated, 'that's a cow.'
'Tao,' he insisted with a slight edge in his voice.
'Cow,' I tried again.

He didn't bother repeating himself, having concluded that I was an embarrassingly dim student. Not worth his trouble. As we left the cow-patch, I tried a final time.

'Cow? There, Isaac? A cow.'
'Tao.'

I pointed at the next field where a ewe was suckling her lamb.

'And that's a sheep.'

He'd learned 'sheep' by now.

'Tee,' he said, following his rule that every noun starts with 't' and omitting the 'p' because it was too much hassle, especially for a language expert like him.

'Yes, Isaac, but "tee" is also "key." So what's that sheep? Is it "tee"? Because "key" is "tee". So what's a sheep?'

Tee,' he said.
'And what's a key?'
'Tee.'
'OK. You win.'

Age **Two**

Aberystwyth July 2008 (aged 2 yrs, one month) A day earlier he'd ridden in the funicular which he called the 'train up'. Next day, he's crossing the beach on my shoulders and he points to it, hoping for a second ride.

Isaac: Train up. Train up.
Me: Train up sick.
Isaac: Train up better.

I was lying on his bed one evening as he fiddled with something by the chest of drawers. I couldn't see what.

Isaac: Isaac fix it.
Me: What?
Isaac: Isaac fix wind-blow.

(Electric fan)

The dustcart is 'lorry-bin.' An automated road-sweeping machine is 'man drive mop.' He calls the Palm Tree pub the 'house all red' because the windows glow orange in the dark. I asked if he wanted to go to the 'house all red' for a beer and he called it the 'house all beer.'

Nov 21st 2008 (aged 2 yrs, 5 months) I tried to teach him 'tomorrow.' He said 'morrow' twice. I emphasised it. '*To*morrow.'

[Nothing]

Me: *To*morrow.

No response. I repeated it again. Finally, he said, '*To* morrow. No more' ... meaning 'stop.'

December 14th He's started to use 'OK.' He happily said 'Mairkiss-mess' to strangers and family alike. But this took some prompting from me. He learned within a few days that Fr Christmas ('Far Kiss-mess') is 'Santa.' I caught him practising with a doll Santa, saying 'present please.'

He says 'leave it' to urge an end to unwelcome action, e.g. being tickled. 'Daddy doing' means 'what are you doing?' But he says 'daddy doing' without an upward inflection.

He has a name for Ken (the driver of his Grandpa, Peter Pilkington) 'Onj Ganpa' on account of Ken's red jacket. Then he gave him a new name 'Red Ganpa.' Then 'Red Ken.'

He has a rag and a dummy (comforter). He recently stopped saying 'dummy gone' and 'raggie gone.' Instead he said 'raggy-dummy.' That's a command. 'Raggy-dummy' means I must find his raggy and dummy.

I woke him after his nap and he said 'big bottle gone.' Then, reaching round behind him, he said 'got it.'

December 29th (aged 2 yrs, 6 months) Returning from Somerset. He played on a ledge in the crowded train and jumped off into my arms. It was hard work and he sensed I would soon tire of catching him after each jump. Normally, to conclude a game, I say 'one more time.' He pre-empted me:

'No one more time.'

He said this each time I helped him onto the ledge.

January 6th 2009 He finished some blueberries & wanted more.

Isaac: More?
Me: You've finished them.
Isaac: Shop. Get it.

Isaac on manners. He finishes his apple juice and offers me the empty cup.

Isaac: More?

As I depart for the kitchen.

Me: Say please.
Isaac: Please. [Pause] Thank-you later.

Jan 11th 2009 I change a very full nappy.

Isaac: See poo. See poo please.
Me (to myself): That is an almighty poo.
Isaac: See nighty poo.

While he performs an action he gives a running commentary. This has changed lately. Instead of 'Isaac do it' or 'my do it' he says 'I do it.' It's unclear if 'I' is a pronoun or a contraction of 'Isaac.'

The playground. We left with his bone-shaker bike & I hoped he'd ride it to the boundary of the park. But he gave up as soon as we were out of the playground. He said 'hard work.'

Meaning he's tired or can't be bothered to do something.

We held a negotiation during which he used the word 'carrit' a lot – 'carry it' meaning 'carry me.' I took the bike in one hand and hoisted him onto my shoulders, steadying him with my free hand, and started the trek home.

Isaac from above: 'Hard work.'

If a journey lasts more than a few minutes, he says 'long way.' A longer walk is 'long way long way.' When the walk ends: 'no long way.'

Celia phoned Grandpa Peter while Isaac played with the DVD buttons. Celia asked Isaac to speak to Grandpa.

Isaac: Busy. Busy.

I showed him a picture book with a toolbox and a 'spanner.' He said 'panner.' I said 'spanner.' He said 'panner.' I said, 'not panner. Sssspanner. Say sssssssssspanner.' He copied it exactly. 'Sssssssssspanner.'

New phrases today. 'Ice melted' and 'I need it.' Celia says she's heard both of those ages ago. She always says that.

After a race around the park, he wanted his raggy and dummy.

Isaac: Raggy-dummy!
Me: Where's the dummy gone?
Isaac: Dummy hiding outside.
Me: Oh, is it? Shall I go outside and find it?
Isaac: Yeah, please, OK.

Celia dragged him away from the DVD player.

Isaac: More press button.

At noon.

Me: What do you want for lunch?
Isaac: Doctor Who.

Bath-time. Making fake phone calls, with the plug as a phone, he says 'doctor peaking.' To finish the call, he says 'goodbye, see you later.'

Jan 24th 2009 (aged 2 yrs, 7 months) He started to say 'can.' I was changing his nappy and instead of 'Isaac see poo' he said 'Isaac can see poo.'

Turning the TV away from me, he says ‘no Daddy can see telly.’

He’s started to say ‘need’ in the last few days. ‘Need’ and ‘can’ arrived together.

Jan 31st 2009 He says ‘I want’ and ‘I’ll do this’ for the first time. And ‘go way’ to end unwelcome action instead of ‘leave it.’

Beginning to count to ten. He always omits four. He’s coined a new term ‘two-three-five’ which means ‘several.’ When he spots playthings in moderate numbers e.g. Lego pieces, he says ‘two-three-five Lego.’ The rubber bath-mat has plastic suckers which fall off and look like snails. Several snails are ‘two-three-five snails.’ To count to ten he says ‘one, two-three-five, six, seven, eight, nine, ten’ so the phrase ‘two-three-five’ is wired into his brain. He can’t insert ‘four.’ (This difficulty lasted a few weeks and vanished.)

Feb 2nd 2009 He uses a plural. ‘Aeroplane’ he said, pointing to a plane in a book. He turned the page. ‘More aeroplanes.’ He definitely understood the difference.

Same day. First use of ‘why’ but without an upward inflection. I was getting dressed in the bathroom.

Isaac: Daddy doing pants on.
Me: We say ‘putting.’ Daddy ‘putting’ pants on.
Isaac: Why.

He said ‘why’ in a flat tone, without a question mark.

Me: We just do.
Isaac: Putting. Daddy putting pants on.

Feb 3rd 2009 Long day. We went to church, then to Browns Hotel with Grandpa and Nuala for my dad’s 80th. He called Browns ‘Grandpa house.’ Then he conceded that it was a ‘café.’ An expensive cafe! I tried doing roly-poly on the cushions at Browns to tire him out. Didn't work. I was simply irritating the entire tea-room. I wanted to stop. I said to Isaac, 'one more time?'

Isaac: No one more time. All day long.

Nuala grabbed him and plonked him on her knee. He became instantly distressed. A huge flashback to the moment when I first took him to Weatherill nursery and left him there. 'No Daddy going! No Daddy going!' he said in horror and distress. I had to take him from Nuala. He wept and needed much reassurance before he settled. Back home, confidentially, he said:

Isaac: No be quiet here.
Me: No. No be quiet here.
Isaac: Be quiet in church.
Me: Yes.

He thought Browns Hotel was as bad as church.

He now delivers quite complex sentences regularly, e.g. 'I can do it' or 'I want this.'

Today, while using a towel to play monsters: 'Daddy help Isaac be monster please.'

Pointing to the spot where the rocking-horse hurt him earlier. 'Isaac ow here, member?' [remember]

Feb 4th 2009 He wants to look for his raggie so I go 'upladder' (upstairs.)

Isaac: Upladder. Upladder somewhere.

First use of 'somewhere' pronounced 'sum air.' Simple things are becoming easier. 'Where's raggie?' he said this morning, Feb 5th, instead of 'raggie gone.'

He scolds a toy called Monkey.

Isaac: Be naughty. Go way. Time out.

Confusion/fascination over 'this' and 'that.' Typical monologue: 'dis one, that one. Dis. ... this monster. That monster.' He wears socks on his hands when going outside. 'Hand-socks.'

Two minutes with Isaac. **Feb 5th 2009.** Morning.

Isaac wearing hand-socks. Takes Monkey.

Isaac: Monkey, monkey, ahhh. Sorry. Sit down. Sit down. OK. No. In cage. No. Now. In cage now.

(Gets fireguard, places it over Monkey on floor.)

Isaac: Now. Now. In. In now. Now. Keep going. Keep going. Hello. I in cage.

(Tries to get into the cage. He doesn't fit.)

Isaac: No. This Monkey cage.

(Replaces fireguard in front of fire.)

Isaac: Doing. This.

(Picks up fire tongs.)

Isaac: Pick up.

(Picks up Monkey with tongs.)

Isaac: Pick up. Look. Look Daddy. Look. Funny. Funny?

(Approaches me with Monkey in tongs and puts Monkey on the table.)

Isaac: Play football?

(Gets football. Puts football under fireguard.)

Isaac: In cage. Hello, ball.

(Picks up Little Teddy with tongs.)

Isaac: Little Teddy, Little Teddy, Little Teddy. Ah. Baby Teddy.

(Abandons Little Teddy. Takes socks off his hands)

Isaac: Careful.

(Picks up Sad Teddy)

Isaac: Ah. Get. In cage.

(Sits down with Sad Teddy and watches TV)

Later. I cycled him home from Weatherill nursery, dummy in his mouth, and I ordered him not to drop the dummy. It was snowy and there was no chance I could pick up a dummy with him in the child seat. When we got back he fished for a reward.

Isaac: No dummy drop it.
Feb 6th He wants to be lifted up to press the light switch.

Isaac: Really big high one.

New word today – 'fine.' He was on the bed stacking the pillows near the footrest so as not to hurt himself while jumping. It was hard work for him. 'Heavy?' I asked.

'No,' he huffed, dumping another pillow. 'Fine.'

He's started calling me 'Lloyd' as he's realised it gets my attention quicker than the usual 'Daddy! Daddy doing. Daddy c'mere!' He was in the bath when Celia came home and he called out 'Seals' – her family nickname. He does this especially when he wants her to come upstairs.

When I unplug the bath he pleads for 'more bath little bit' or 'little bit more.' But he never sticks to the bargain. It's always, 'little bit more.'

Feb 14th 2009 Celia on phone to Grandpa Peter explaining Isaac's increasing bossiness.

Celia: He's totally in charge.

Isaac overhears.

Isaac. In charge. Isaac in charge.

Feb 15th He says 'there tis' whenever we're looking for something. He joined us searching the house for a lost item and he shouted 'there tis' thinking that the point of the hunt was to shout 'there tis' a lot. He didn't realise that the searchers must shout 'there tis' only when the object has been found.

In his room, I found him attacking the wall with his plastic screwdriver.

Me: Isaac?
Isaac: Fixing busy.

Then he said, 'busy fixing.' Interchangeable as yet.

New word. Feb 21st in bath, asking to be given a toy duck I was filling with water.

'Isaac by self.'

Feb 22nd He was being noisy on the 205 bus which terminates at Paddington station. I asked him to shush. 'Too noisy,' I said. He carried on shouting and said 'people like it.'
He's mesmerised by the automatic announcement on the bus. '205 to Paddington.' He echoed 'Paddington' with delight whenever he heard it. Which was every single stop along the six-mile journey.

Big leap forward in recent days. A greater sense of self. He says, 'me' more often but still 'Isaac' to refer to himself. Seeing his toy bike in the garden.

'Get it ... (pause) ... for me.'

He says 'where' quite often but it's always 'wheresa' as in 'wheresa biscuit?', 'wheresa dummy?', 'wheresa raggie-dummy?'

Cycling back from the park on his blue plastic bike. 'I do it. By myself.'

He now says 'mend it' as well as 'fix it.'

Feb 28th 2009 (aged 2 yrs, 8 months) Evening. Isaac suddenly turns and points.

'How old are you?'

This seemed a massive leap forward. A sense of self coupled to a realisation that I'm not part of the furniture or a feature, like the moon, but an individual. I told him my age – 45. He heard it and repeated it 'four two five.' Then he asked Celia the same question. '39'. He pronounced it correctly.

March 2nd I came home. Workmen in the house, Celia in the kitchen, Isaac on the sofa. I asked what he'd been doing.

'Mummy naughty.'
'Was Mummy naughty? What was she doing?'
'Bashing.'
'Bashing who?
'Isaac.'

Complete fiction and done in a quiet, mischievous smiling voice.

Still craving warm milk and specifying the preparation details. 'Big warm bottle. Want big one. Warm.'

Asking about letters: 'What number dat?'

March 4th 2009 'I want dat. Dis one. Digger please. I want that digger.'

I gave him the digger. After playing for a bit, boredom arrives.

'I want ticking. I want do ticking. (Sticking) I want do ticking please.'

I open the cupboard.

'I want blue. I want this blue.' (glue)

He gets the glue and sits down.

'I want tissue.'

I give him a tissue.
'Scissors. I want scissors. Where's? I want scissors. Green.'

He gets the green scissors.

'I want cut.'

Starts cutting a plastic glove. I look at him.

'Cutting. My glove.'
'Do you want apple juice, Isaac?'
'No. Doing. Do.'

He puts glue all over his hands then wipes it off with a tissue. Then wipes his nose.

'Bash.'

Repeats 'bash.' Takes tissue.
'I put it in bin.'

Runs out. Picks up glue. About to defile the TV screen.

'Isaac. Don't put the glue on the TV.'
'Here?'

He holds the glue to his face.
'OK,' I say.

He puts glue on his face and nose. Wipes it off with another tissue. Puts the glue lid to his mouth.
'Ooh. Funny. Dat funny.'

Picks up a camera.
'Camera. Broken.'

It reminds him of Leo's camera.

'Where's the Leo camera? Leo's. Leo's camera. Wheresa like Leo's camera? Gone. Where's a like Leo's camera gone?'

[Ends]

Before leaving for nursery, I showed him a framed photo of Celia dancing, with her splayed fingers held out. Much fascination from Isaac. I put him on the bike where he could still see the photo. 'Mummy do this,' he said and splayed his fingers like in the photo. I looked back into the room. The photo of Celia was on top of the TV. Before we left he said goodbye. 'Bye-bye mummy. Bye-bye mummy picture.'

Conducting his parents. Standing between us during a musical interlude.

'Mummy song vye-lin, Daddy song tittar.'

(Mummy plays violin, Daddy plays guitar.)

Outside, getting on the bike, referring to an earlier prohibition against him running away from me.

'No run away, Daddy.'
'No. Never,' I said.
'Later.'
'No, not later. Never.'
'Soon.'

A new word!
'Is that your new word? Soon.'

No reply. I put him in the bike seat and set off.

'New word. Soon,' he said, like a Linguaphone record. 'New word. Soon.'

March 10th 2009 New word – 'him.' Everything is 'him' suddenly. No concept of gender. Watching TV. 'Him, pink lady, him.'

March 14th On the tube to Fulham Broadway. A man is leaving the train. Isaac points. 'I love that man.' The man doesn't hear. Gets off. Isaac shrieks in distress. 'Ah-uhhh! Where's he gone?'

March 16th Leo mucking about with a glass of apple juice nearby.

Me: Leo, don't spill it.
Leo: Who's Bill?

Leo with a plastic dinosaur.

Leo: What's this one?
Me: Pterodactyl.
Leo: How you spell it?

I spelled it and he repeated it back to me. He's quick and knows the alphabet, aged 3.

Me: It's a hard one because it starts with a P.
Leo: It starts with a D.
Me: No, it starts with a P.

Leo. It starts with a D. D for dinosaur.

March 22nd 2009 Isaac with Brown teddy. I said he should tell Brown teddy a story.

Isaac: Isaac-Jo went go park over dare, member!

During the last week he's started to say, 'where are you?' as in 'Mummy, where are you?'

Previously, almost invariably, he referred to us in the third person.

March 28th (aged 2 yrs, 9 months) 'Whassat?' constantly.

'Whassat? Wherezat fom? Wherezit fom? Wherezit come fom?'

At the pond, where he fell in six months ago, he warned me to take care. 'No Daddy fall in. Bit cold dat.'

March 30th The park. A dog nicked our ball. Great distress. Afterwards I asked him to tell Mummy what happened. 'What happened?' Celia prompted. He couldn't speak for a moment because he felt sure the story needed to begin with 'happen.' But I think he felt equally sure that was wrong. So he just started, 'happen ... happen.' And eventually he said 'dog' and 'ball' in no coherent order.

I took him to the Olympic park – a building site full of unmanned diggers. 'Stroke digger?' he asked. I showed him the Olympic stadium, half built, black ribs jutting out of the ground.

'That's the Olympic Games. Can you say Olympic Games?
'Pick games.'
'You can do bashing at the Olympic Games. You can bash.'
'With tick?' (with a stick?)

April 4th 2009 Earliest genitive singular that I can recall. He finds me dozing in his room.

'Dat Isaac's bed.' (usually 'Isaac bed')

April 5th At lunch, he points right at me. 'What's your name?'

'Lloyd.'
He turns to Celia.
'What's your name?'
'Celia.'
'Isaac? What's your second name?' I said.
'Two harve,' (two and a half, his age)
'No. It's Evans,' I said. 'Now ask me what my second name is.'
'What's your sename?'
'Evans,' I said.
Isaac: 'No. I'm Evans.'
'Ask Mummy what her second name is.'
'What's your sename?'
'Evans,' she said.
Isaac: 'No, I'm Evans.'

Showing him some picture books, he said 'what's that?' pointing to a photo showing some part of London. I said: 'That's here. That's London.' The picture resembled Arberry Rd, next to ours, and he now thinks 'London' is Arberry Rd. Each time we cycle past it, he says with full confidence, 'that's London.' When we reach our street I say, 'is this London?'

'No, this home,' he says.

For ages afterwards, when I collected him from nursery on the bike, he insisted on 'going down London', i.e. along Arberry Rd. If I refused to 'go down London' he got furious and started thrashing around in his bike seat.

Easter break 'to Grandpa house' in Somerset. Constant questions. 'Woss where going?' but 'where' sometimes sounds like 'we're.'

'Woss we're going?'

As our train crossed London, he identified all the half-finished tower blocks as 'Lympic Games.'

April 13th 2009 We walk to the grave of Helen, Celia's mother. 'Very too long way.'

After Sarah's departure on Easter Sunday. 'Where's Sarah? Where'sy gone? Where Sarah gone?'

Another trip to Helen's grave. I told him this was his other grandma and that she was in the 'tone house' (stone house.) He thought he was seeing Grandma, my mum, whom he always voices as Gan *maaaa*! to signal his awareness that it's a different name from Grandpa. Celia told him that his other grandma had gone.

'Monster eat grandma?' he asked me.
'No,' I said, 'she was sick.'
'Where sick? See sick. See grandma sick.'

Regular new phrase. 'All by myself.'

He observes others making independent actions – 'Daddy do it by self.'

First heard 'not too much' during a bike ride to the Toy Museum in which he complained of 'big bangs' on the back of the bike, i.e. bumps in the road. The Toy Museum used to be 'Toys' but now it's 'Toyzeum.'

Celia has three friends called Sarah. Sarah Hurley, a blonde who wears glasses, is six months pregnant so we call her 'Sarah got baby in tummy' to distinguish her from the others. Isaac started pointing to any bespectacled blonde.

'Dat Sarah got baby in tummy.'

April 24th (aged 2 yrs, 10 months) Isaac begging and pleading for something.

Me: You're playing for the sympathy vote.
Isaac: Whass Zebedee vote?

April 30th 2009 'Not sure' for first time, on way home.

May 1st Isaac farts.

Me: What's that?
Isaac: Helicopter.

May 4th 'Where are we?' instead of 'Woss where going?'

'I'm farmer,' while digging up stones in the garden of the Imperial Hotel, Hythe. Outside the lift at the hotel, returning home. 'No home! No go home!'

Perpetual questions along the lines of -

'Whass that man? Whass ee doing? Whass that man doing?'

May 5th On his tractor outdoors. 'Bit windy. Too bit windy.'

Isaac tells a lie. **May 6th** I'm taking him to bed at 9 pm. The TV announcer previews the next programme. But Isaac knows he can stay up for *Dr Who.*

'Man said *Dr Who* coming.'

May 8th Going to nursery after a long non-nursery weekend. He's reluctant to go.

Isaac: Daddy. Daddy?
Me: Yes.
Isaac: Nursery closed.

It was open.

May 9th On his tractor, discussing whether the tractor was too small for me to go on, he said 'bigger' for the first time. That evening, I took him downstairs to watch *CBeebies* or 'Beebies' as he calls it

Isaac: Might be Beebies. (First instance of 'might be')

May 10th 2009 The pond. Isaac picking grass and throwing it to the ducks which refused to eat grass. 'Daddy tell ducks eat grass.'

Me: Ducks! Eat grass!

Ducks eat no grass.

May 10th The pond. We name a large grey carp 'Freddie. ... Freddie the Fish.' Celia joins us and asks what we're doing.

'Naming the fish,' I say, proudly. 'What's the fish called Isaac?'
'Jonathan.'

May 11th Leo counselling Isaac about not having a dummy.

Leo: No dummy, don't have a dummy, people laugh, they laugh, people laugh. [Beat] Where's my dummy?

May 12th I give him a new truck. Isaac said 'where's it from?' about six times.
I said 'a shop.'

'Where's it from shop? Where's it from that shop? Where's that? Where's ... where's it from that shop? Where's that shop from?'

At the pool. Teaching pool closed. The big pool is too cold. 'Too bit cold. Bit freezing.'

May 21st Park. Men playing rugby. 'Dat egg.'

Picking him up from nursery.

Isaac: Need coat.

Me: No, it's too warm.
Isaac: Tis not warm. Tis cold.

In the last two weeks. 'How about me?' for the first time. 'Not yet' for the first time. Even when it's not true as in, after he's done a poo ...

Me: Have you done a poo?
Isaac: Not yet.

(But he has)

'Shall we?' for the first time, as in 'go in park, shall we?' Also 'how bout me?'

'How bout' gaining ground as an all-purpose question opener. But never used incorrectly. When music starts: 'Whass this song bout?'

May 28th (aged 2 yrs, 11 months) He hears about a forthcoming holiday involving a ferry. 'Go in big boat. Tractor come in big boat? Windy come. Blow big boat in sea.'

May 30th He discusses his birthday party with a puppet called Tigger.

'You're can come in my party.'
'When's your party Isaac?' I ask.
Long pause.
'My party ... downladder.' (downstairs)

Isaac makes a joke.

Me: What's your favourite type of sandwich?
Isaac: Poo.

Me: What colour's your hair, Isaac?'
Isaac: Grey.
Me: No, it's blond.

Isaac: Blond.
Me: Like yellow.
Isaac: Lellow.

Like my friend Greg who said 'lellow' in 1966!

Isaac: I got some cream. Look my hands. Look come see brick. I do some numbers. Do some number.

June 1st At home. Leo: 'I'm nearly a lady.'

Leo also says, 'sometimes I'm a girl called Nicola.'

Isaac tries to bash Leo.

Leo: I'm not your best friend. I'm not talking to you. I'm talking to Lloyd.

Isaac tries to regain control of the situation.

Isaac: I'm talking to ... Lloyd. Daddy. I'm talking to Daddy.

'Lovely day' started at least a month ago. Typical use: 'Lovely day this. Bit rainy.'

New phrase to stop unwelcome action. Instead of 'leave it' he says 'no like this.' But on May 28th he said 'don't' for the first time in a sentence taking the form 'no ...' followed by a description of the action he sought to curtail.

'No don't do this ... tickle me.'

I selected *don't* for praise.

Me: Isaac! Well done. You said 'don't.'
Isaac: Who's 'don't'?

Leo seeing me hug Celia. Leo: 'That's nice. Look at them. Take a picture. Say cheese.'

June 2nd 2009 Isaac takes a note-book and asks me to order food, as in a restaurant. I think he believes waiters draw the food when they take orders. So he draws the food. But first he tootles around with a balloon and a pump.

Isaac: Who's that balloon? Need pump. Need pump. In balloon. Put pump in balloon. I know. I know.

Picks up turquoise suitcase.

Isaac: Where's my bag. Look my bag, look my bag. Look my bag. Dat very pretty bag. Very pretty bag. What's it working, what's your want Daddy? What's your want? Your want some tea?
Me: Yes.
Isaac: OK.

He takes notebook from suitcase. Draws.

Isaac: I'm drawing some tea. Where's tea gone? This is fun. I'm drawing your tea, look your tea go round a round a round. Your tea. Dere your tea. Your tea. Dere your tea. Look your tea.
Me: That's nice.
Isaac: No more tea. (Picks up landline.) Hello, yeah, yeah, yeah, all finished. Yes yes yes. Tea. Teas. All teas. Yes, yes. Ice diss teas. Yes, yes. Teas. I try that. OK, see yer bye. That was driver train. We do some crayon. What's your want, Daddy?
Me: Sandwich please.
Isaac: Sandwich OK. (Drawing) Done sandwich! Put these in my bag. [On phone] Hello, yeah, yeah, yeah, yes, yes, on train. Put my bag. Yes, yes, yes, just at home. Yes, yes. OK. See yer bye. That was doctor. He said, don't know. He said, often face-shun (operation.) Giraffe is often face-shun. Hello, often face-shun. Sit down. Sit down, often face-shun. Often face-shun. [Phone] OK yes, yes, yes, OK see yer bye.

He approaches me with notebook.

Isaac: What's your want, Daddy?
Me: Marmite.
Isaac: Jam. And bread. I'm drawing some bread. This not bread. Whass I like? Whass your like? This is one. This is one. White. White. Often face-shun. Marmite jam. This Marmite jam.
Me: Is it?
Isaac: Yeah (on phone) Hello. Hello. Yes, yeah yeah yeah yeah. OK. I'm Isaac Mummy Daddy. With Isaac, Daddy. Yeah yeah yeah. Yes. Yes.

Sings 'Yes, yes, yes' to tune of *Ba Ba Black Sheep.*

Isaac. Yes, I'm playing some balloons. See yer. Bye. See yer. Bye. Big boy's pants. Big boy's pants.

Picks up ball.

Isaac: Big watch. Catch. (Throws ball, ball disappears.) Need go now. Need go now. I'm putting. (Puts things in bag.) Thank you. All gone. Need my toys. (Takes car.) Put it in oven. Bye. Putting car in oven.

He exits to kitchen, hears washing machine, is unsettled by the spin-cycle.

Isaac: Bit noisy in kitchen. Bit noisy in kitchen. Bit noisy. Bit noisy in kitchen.
Me: Did you put the car in the oven?
Isaac: No. Bit. Cos. Bit noisy. Car. No put car in ... what's your want Daddy?
Me: Big bowl of soup.
Isaac: No. Giraffe doing it. Ooh my bag. What's that? Elephant. (Consoles toy Giraffe.) Oh your bottom's out. Don't worry. Don't worry. Just a minute.

Gets stethoscope.

Me: What've you got there Isaac?
Isaac: Tethscope. (Applies it to Giraffe.) Dat. All better. All better.

June 3rd 2009 Watching a boy genius on TV playing the piano.

Me: Would you like to play the piano like that?
Isaac: Yes. Need go shop get one. Little one. Little one please. And chair.

The park. Me phoning PR people for theatre tickets. 'Whass your doing?'

'I'm fixing up theatre.'
'What bout me, what bout me fix up theatre?'

June 6th Teeming with rain. Isaac on floor. 'Tis not lovely day outside.'

Later, outdoors, Isaac in conversation with another small boy with a blue scooter.

Isaac: What's your name?
Max: Max.
Isaac: What's that?
Max: Scooter.

Pause.

Isaac: It's all blue.

Isaac starts to say 'What's your name' again but stops after 'What's your ...' realising that he's already asked it. Max takes up the reins.

Max: I haven't dot, I haven't dot, I haven't dot ... helmet.

June 20th To Grandpa's house. He asks if his cousin Jo will be there.

Isaac: See Jo?
Me: No.

Isaac: Where Jo?
Me: In Wales.
Isaac: What's Wales?
Me: It's a country. Where Jo lives.
Isaac: Where's Wales gone?

June 22nd 2009 The eve of his third birthday. Presents on the dresser. We won't let him open them. 'I want ope my presents.'

'You can't, Isaac.'
'Try!' he said.
'No.'
'Look and see?'
'No!'

He likes his two new phrases, 'try' and 'look and see.'

Age Three

June 23rd 2009 We sing *Happy Birthday*. 'Isaac, how old are you?'

'Two harve.'
'No.'
'Nearly three.'
'No. You are three.'
'Am are three.'

He likes 'am are' instead of 'I am.' When told he's not in charge, he says 'am are in charge.' He has trouble using 'you' in a phrase. He prefers 'your.'

'Your can do it' when asking me to perform tasks (which is a statement not a command, interestingly.)

June 24th 2009 First use of 'yesterday' whilst putting Playdoh on his lip like a moustache.

'I like a man, show Mummy yesterday, member?'

Referring to a workman.

First use of 'there you are' after finding *CBeebies* with the TV remote.

June 26th Aberystwyth. Growing awareness of place and space and of different functions for different locations. At the bus-station, I went to check bus-times. I came back to Celia and Isaac. 'What you're doing over there?' he said. He wanted his 'big warm' (bottle) heated up. I said we couldn't because the hotel room has no kitchen.

'Have kitchen downstairs warm up.'

Later – 'kitchen have breakfast.'

Different locations, different functions. New realisations!

Train. He saw writing over the carriage door which he assumed was the train number.

'What number this train have?'
'It doesn't have a number.'
'Tis have.'

We saw my mum looking ill and decrepit on June 27th. I went to see her alone on 28th June. When I returned he asked 'your mum dead?' Which, from a grammatical viewpoint, is the first time he called her anything other than 'Grandma.' Probably he heard me say 'my mum' to Celia. Growing awareness that elements of the world have associations that don't involve him.

Isaac was scared of going into the sea in case he got eaten by fish.

July 4th London. A boat goes up the canal.

Isaac: Where's boat going?
Me: Shops.
Isaac: Not going to shops, going to house.
Me: Is it?
Isaac: Boat-house. Some boats go underwater.
Me: Yes!

I was thrilled by this. 'Some boats go underwater.' Isaac had discovered submarines. I wanted him to say 'submarine.'

Me: What are underwater boats called?
Isaac: Fish.

July 12th 2009 Still saying 'am are three' when asked his age. But no longer 'leave it' or 'go way' when halting an unwanted action. Now it's 'don't do that.'

Urging me to go into a pub to get him apple juice.

'You go,' I said.
'I'm bit little.'

July 13th Isaac finds me using the laptop which for him means two amusements: either watching Michael Jackson videos or doing 'numbers' i.e. typing out huge blocks of letters.

Isaac: Want see Michael Jackson.
Me: Well you can't ...you know why.
Isaac: He's dead.
Me: Yup.
Isaac: He's underneath. He's right down in the grass. He's dead. Are numbers dead?
Me: No.
Isaac: They're better. Want see numbers now.

July 18th He said 'came', past tense of 'come', for the first time. After cutting his lip he said 'blood coming.' The bleeding stopped but restarted. 'Blood came.'

Looking for the remote control, he said 'Michael Jackson take it.' A joke.

July 20th Another joke. He looked straight at me and said 'you're Mummy.'

Celia with Isaac, chatting and changing a nappy.

Celia: I hope not.
Isaac: What's 'hope not'?
Celia: I wish it won't.
Isaac: What's 'wish it won't'?
Celia: Urgh! It's disgusting.
Isaac: It's gusting.

July 21st

Isaac: Michael Jackson dead.
Me: Yes.
Isaac: What's he dead for?

He's concerned about death and assures himself that the dead awaken. Several times he says 'when people dead they turn into monsters.' I say yes since this prospect doesn't alarm him.

Listening to Celia on the phone to Peter (Grandpa).

Isaac: That Mummy's daddy.

25th July 2009 (aged 3 yrs, one month) Questions arriving in a negative form: 'Don't I get a teddy?'

'Where's Daddy then, Daddy in bed, then?'

'Leo's coming round' instead of 'Leo coming.'

Discussing the sea. 'Don't want to go down in the sea. Fish eat me. And sharks. Sometimes they're nice. Sometimes.'

July 26th Watching a Michael Jackson film, including the baby-dangling incident, Isaac reacts sternly.

Isaac: He put baby over the gate. Make him fall over. Naughty old Michael Jackson. Silly old Michael Jackson.

Talking to Paddington about a holiday, Isaac plays the roles of himself and Paddington.

Paddington: Who's flying the plane?
Isaac: Not me.
Paddington: What are we going to do on holiday?
Isaac: We're do some drawing. We can share. You got no hands. You got just arms.

Aug 5th Listening to someone on *CBeebies* talking about a 'problem.'

'Woss ploblem?'

Aug 8th Still asking questions in the negative. 'Can't I have big warm?' [milk]

He often adds a pessimistic flavour to a request as if expecting disappointment. He asks for 'fixing tray' (a plastic box full of tools) so he can play with the tools.

'Can't I have fixing tray? Mummy say no.' He assumes that I'll want to be more generous than Celia.

Aug 6th 2009 First use of 'dipped.' Usually when dipping toast in his egg he says 'I dip it' or 'I'm dipping.' Today – 'I dipped it.'

August 7th Science Museum. Looking at rockets.

Isaac: This space-ship house?
Me: Yes.
Isaac: What space-ship food?
Me: Petrol.

Hyde Park.

Isaac: This very pretty. Flowers pretty. You like flowers?
Me: No, I think flowers bit boring.
Isaac: Flowers not bit boring. Flowers beautiful.

After a while. 'This like jungle.'

Seeing a statue of a man on a horse.

'There's a man on a horse there. Woss man on a horse for?'
'He's hunting.'
'Woss he hunting for?'

'He's hunting foxes'
'Woss he hunting foxes for?'
'He's hunting foxes to get rid of them?'
'Woss he hunting foxes to get ridda dem for?'
Etc.

Picking a handful of blackberries, I pass him a few. 'I want alder dem.'

He's told to get out of the bath. 'Five more minutes and that's it.'

Aug 8th Going to see Sarah Hurley's baby, aged 10 days, he asked if the baby would play football. We said the baby was small but would get bigger. He was disappointed it didn't get bigger while he was there.

Manipulative Isaac. **August 9th** Canal. An old man on a scooter plays *Hey Jude* through a ghetto-blaster. A crisp bag passes. Isaac knows crisps are available in the pub but I've already declined this request. The empty crisp bag blows past.

Isaac: Do you love me?
Me: Of course I love you.
Isaac: I like crisps.
Me: Do you?
Isaac: They're my fwave-wit.

He grabs the empty crisp bag, asks for permission to throw it in the canal, or 'the pond' as he calls it. Permission denied. He does it anyway. I rebuke him mildly. When reproached he always responds, 'go *way*.'

The previous day I'd shown him the 'sunset.' He remembered it but couldn't get the word right. Pointing to the west he said 'there's sunt.'

He still uses 'am are' instead of 'I am' for emphasis. This originated on his birthday.

Me: How old are you?
Isaac: Two harve.
Me: Three. Now you are three.
Isaac: Am are three.

After some encouragement he says 'I am' not 'am are.' He sometimes varies this with 'I'm are' or 'I'm am.'

Aug 21st 2009 After reciting *Humpty Dumpty* for the first time, with some help, he sings:

'All the king's horses and all the king's men/
Couldn't put Humpty together again/
Got to go to hospital.'

A visit to Jane, Celia's aunt. Isaac referred to her as 'Mummy's friend.' He realised there was a connection with Celia's mother. After returning, we were talking about Jane. 'Mummy's friend!' But it's beyond him to grasp that Jane is his mum's mum's sister.

Outside the Palm Tree pub.

'Where's Mummy's mum?'
'She died. She's in the ground.'
Isaac looks to the ground. Points.
'She's in there?'
'Yes. Sort of.'
Head down.
'WAKE UP!! WAKE UP!!

Having schooled him to expect a computer (poota) as a present from Marion and Cousin Jo, I rehearsed him in advance.

'Who are you going to see today?'

'Jo.'
'And?'
'Marion.'
'And she's got a present. What's the present?'
'Might be is a digger.'

Increasing awareness of wider world. 'Jo my cousin. I've got lots of cousins. Tomos my cousin. Rudi my cousin. Django my cousin.'

Male cousins – he omits Oriel and Tabi – but also leaves out Sion.

August 31st 2009 (aged 3 yrs, 2 months) Somerset. Helen's grave. (Celia's mother.)

'Why's she in ground?'
'She was sick.'
'Who made her sick?'

I didn't answer that. He wanted to raise the gravestone and see her. 'Lift her up. You help.' I pretended to help. Isaac pretended to have succeeded. 'I can see her!' Then realising he couldn't shift the stone he said, 'I want to see her eyes.'

Later, with Peter (Grandpa) watching uncomfortably, Isaac spoke about Peter's late wife.

Isaac: Mummy's mum is in the ground.
Peter: What?
Isaac: They put a rock on her. Put a stone on her. She wake up later.

Isaac's only understanding of money is 'twenty pound.' He thinks everything costs 'twenty pound.' I bought him a toy for 50p and made him pay at the till. Later I asked, 'how much did you pay for that?' All he could remember was 'pee.' I told him '50p.'

Later.

Me: How much did the toy cost?
Isaac: Pound pee.

I told him the computer cable provides the computer with food. He was interested in the computer's diet. 'Does it have marmalade?'

Confusion over directions while cycling home.

Me: This way.
Isaac: That the wrong way.
Me: No, this is the right way.
Isaac: No, this is the right way. That's the left way.

Kissing me with stubble. 'Daddy got tickle face.'

Sept 20th 2009 'I found this' he says. He's got hold of my wallet. 'Can't I have it a tiny bit?'

'OK,' I said.
'You have this when you go for a bank.'

Getting more colloquial. 'I don't know' comes out as 'I don't really know.'

About to receive plastic armour and a sword from Auntie Sarah. I explain that armour protects you against the pain of a sword. 'Has it got stinging nettles?'

Trouble with prepositions. 'Mummy's out work.' 'I spit out you.' 'I hide to you.'

He says 'falled' and 'camed.'

More colloquial: 'I don't know, though.' After being accused of kicking Rita, the cat. 'I didn't kick her, I shoed her.'

Seeing the gorillas in London Zoo.

'Are they happy or sad?'

'Sad.'

Seeing the lions.

'Happy or sad?'
'Sad.'
'Why?'
'Can't get out.'

Oct 4th Sunday 2009 (aged 3 yrs, 3 months) Hurts his thumb. 'I can't go to church-school because I hurt my thumb.'

An obsession with becoming older. Seeing me take Aspirin. 'When I big I can have that.'

He was told he could clean the fireplace when he got bigger. 'After I get bigger and bigger I get very little.' He sees growth and shrinkage as a natural cycle. Magnification then diminution.

Describing the purpose of tools. 'I need my umbrella when my hair doesn't go all sprinkly.' ('when' for 'so.')

'I want dinosaur robot for Christmas. Mote control robot.'

He talks of 'mote control' this and that. Much excitement about Leo's party. Dropping him at Leo's the day before the party.

Me: We're going to Leo's party tomorrow.
Isaac: Are you coming?
Me: Yes.
Isaac: Mummy coming?
Me: Yes.
Isaac: Is buggy coming?
Me: Yes.
Isaac: Not dummy!

He's ashamed of his dummy in public

At the party, a young female clown:

Clown: Do you know why I'm here? Who knows why I'm here?
Isaac: Cos you're lovely.

October 20th 2009 Isaac on girls. 'Don't like babies cos they're a bit little. Don't like girls.'
'Why?'
'I just don't.'

The park, before the arrival of Nuala and Grandpa.

Isaac: Maybe Nuala's there.
Me: OK.
Isaac: Might be she's got a present.
Me: Well, I don't know. She may not have one.
Isaac: What's it going to be?
Me: I don't know.
Isaac: Might be Nuala's there.
Me: Why are you so keen to see Grandpa and Nuala?
Isaac: Cos I love dem.

Anticipating an intercom game with Leo. 'That's might be going to be great fun.' I said 'yes.' Isaac said, 'what's great fun?'

New game: asking why things exist. 'What's lights for, what's taps for, what's ducks for?' So I asked 'what's questions for?' He said 'telling things.'

Oct 29th 2009 (aged 3 yrs, 4 months) Owl's head got broken.

Isaac: Maybe get some glue to fix it. From the shop. I'm going get some glue tomorrow.

Lying in bed, he crossed his legs and asked me to climb onto his ankle so he could give me a ride, like I do with him. 'I'm too big,' I said. 'When you bit little you can do it.'

He thinks he'll be big one day and I'll be little.

'Oh I see!' I said.
'What's I see? Why you say, I see? What's I see?'
'It means "I understand."'

He didn't understand.

Morning play. Covering several minutes. He sits with white bear and shows him how to write.

Isaac: This is the O, O, O, O, wer, we're, wer, wash your hands, where's everybody, they gone home, OK. When's my friend come back? Going get your mummy, show me other page, other page, it said wer, wer wer, go wash your hands, where's everybody, oh. They gone home, oh, I need to see, everybody. Everybody's just here. I'm watch him, what's your name? What's your mummy's mummy ...

(writes in a book, pulls out page)

Isaac: Yeah, did it. Let's talk for. Your mummy. I'm going to leave it to ... it's dry now. Yeah.

(puts page by TV)

Isaac: It going to get dry in a minute. Everybody read. Going to read you a book.

(comes to me)

Isaac: Can I going to get a book please? Got a get a book.

(I check shelf, he spots jigsaw)

Isaac: What's the pieces? Can't I have the pieces? Who gave me this to a?

(takes jigsaw to white bear, starts taking Sellotape off the box, puts it on sofa)

Isaac: Put up here, don't want a messy book. Getting it off. Want a mess, don't we. Play games for your presents, you get peller, polar bear, it's polar, it's your birthday, when's your birthday? In June. When's mine in June. In the, in school, I'm going to open it now, put the mess on here, don't we. Don't we.

(opens jigsaw, puts pieces in two plastic bags)

Isaac: We got to, we got to, all these pieces, why they not little, in a minute, they all pieces, we need ... like these, I like these.

(fails to open bag, opens it with his teeth, makes a hole, tips pieces onto floor)

Isaac: See, see, where these are O, O, I did tell the pieces your birthday, silly old pieces, what do you want to do? OK. A bin.

(puts empty plastic bags on his hands, like gloves)

Isaac: All ready to go.

(starts putting pieces into the box)

Isaac: Cos we don't all der dem. Pieces. These are my hands. What's, what's it, in the bag, my hands, silly old you, my hands, oh, I put it in there, in here, when I go hurt myself.

(takes bags off hands, gets scissors, starts cutting bags)

Isaac: Oh that's why I cut ... oh ... (comes to me.) That one's broken.
Me: Did you bite a hole in it?
Isaac: No, I didn't.

(Bursts into tears)

Nov 5th 2009 About to leave for Exeter. Celia is dressed in a symphony of grey and pink.

Me: Does Mummy look pretty?

Isaac: Yes. She looks like a robot. Sterminate, sterminate.

Her grey dress reminds him of a Dalek.

Nov 7th Isaac sings.

Two fat sausages sitting in a pan/
One went pop and the other went bang/
No more sausages sitting in a pan.

Nov 14th Isaac says 'I did talk to Grandpa. He said, *Hello Isaac.*'

Me: Where is he?
Isaac: Out his home.
Me: Where is it?
Isaac: Where's his phone? He's very fat. He's very old.

Nov 20th Passing a skip full of bricks. I pause, looking for firewood.

Isaac: Whass you want bricks for?
Me: I don't want bricks
Isaac: Whass you doesn't want bricks for?

Later, with a plastic Dalek.

Isaac: Whass inside him?
Me: A monster.

We open the Dalek. No monster.

Isaac: You told me there was a monster in him.
Me: Yeah, sorry. I lied.
Isaac: Who didn't put a monster in him? Shall we put a battery in him?
Me: Doesn't make any difference.
Isaac: Shall we, shall we, shall we, shall we try ...
Me: It doesn't take batteries.

Isaac: Shall we try, are we got some battery, shall we try, are we got some battery, shall we try and find, shall we try for, we can look, yeah?
Me: It doesn't take batteries.
Isaac: The Dalek does have a battery in Doctor Who.

Exits & returns from kitchen with battery.

Isaac: I got some. I got one. One. We have. See. I'm going to put it. In here. OK. We haven't got the right ones.

Exits to kitchen & brings smaller batteries.

Isaac: There. We got some. These are the right batteries. Kay? Here they are. Here one. One, two. There, there maybe it going work now. Here wah then. Here is. Kay. Here are the strew [Brings four screws]. Here are, here are these, here are they, here they are. The strew, the strewdriver. Here is. The strewdriver, the strewdriver.
Me: Where is it?
Isaac: I can't find it. Might be it does have, maybe it does it have one, maybe it's got like that. Strewdriver. Where are you? Where's?

He forces me to put batteries inside the Dalek. He puts in two then removes one.

Isaac: Might be it going to work with one battery in it.
Me: I assure you it won't.
Isaac: Might be it does OK?

Plays with Dalek.

Isaac: I got a monster inside me. (Giggles) Ha ha ha I going to shoot you. I going to shoot you ha ha ha. I got a monster inside, ha ha ha. Don't shoot me, don't shoot me, don't shoot me. (Explosion) I going to get that Ninja Turtle aha ha ha ha. He going to shoot you. Ha ha ha. He going to shoot you.

Nov 27th (aged 3 years, 5 months) A day at Celia's office. He calls this 'out Mummy's work' ('out' for 'at.') He comes home. 'I like it out Mummy's work. You can't touch anything. ... You can come to our work. You can't touch anything.'

Celia has a sore throat & he claims the same affliction. 'I've got a crackly voice. ... I haven't got a voice.'

Eating his first Polo mint.

Isaac: What's it got a hole? Uh? Ahh?
Me: I don't know.
Isaac: I did clean my teeth. Mummy? Daddy. I want to watch Michael Jackson. They're very juicy. Please can I sit on your knee.

Nov 28th 2009 Names a new toy 'Anglozander.' His attempt at Alexander. At St Paul's school, he talks to Anglozander. I play the role of Anglozander.

Isaac: Are you coming to my school?
Me (as Anglozander): No. I haven't got a brain. Have you got a brain?
Isaac: Yes.

He points to his head.

Me: Where's your brain?
Isaac: In my bottom!

He runs around shouting 'in my bottom!'

Recently he's stopped saying 'can't I...' at the start of every sentence. He's begun to prefix nouns with 'know' which is short for 'you know.' Asked what he wants for Christmas, he says, 'mote control dine-saw and mote control robot.'

December 3rd The Santa conundrum.

Celia: Some children say Fr Christmas isn't real. What would you say to children who say Fr Christmas isn't real?
Isaac: I'd say dey wadn't real.

Dec 28th (aged 3 yrs, 6 months)

Isaac: Rain makes ice melt. I know lots of things. And Leo knows lots of numbers.

Watching the opening sequence of *Bolt* with Bolt as a little dog.

Isaac: Can I have a dog like Bolt?
Me: No, we've got a cat and they'd fight.
Isaac: You can have a cat. And I can have a dog and we can all sing together.

Best question over Christmas 2009: 'What's that cow standing up for?'

Jan 10th 2010 Frozen pond. Walking on it, we're yelled at by a dog-walking woman. Later we see her again.

Me: Mad old bat.
Isaac: Mandol bat, shall we chop her head off?
Me: No, she might need it later.
Isaac: Shall we throw her in the bin?

He becomes obsessed by exposed bits of pavement.

Isaac: Who did that crack?
Me: I don't know.

Later, by holes in the canal ice.

Isaac: Who did that hole?
Me: I don't know.
Isaac: People.
Me: Was it?

Isaac: They stand on their skis.

Later

Isaac: Why you doesn't know things?
Me: I don't know everything.
Isaac: Mummy knows everything.
Me: Hmm.

Seeing another crack.

Isaac: Who did that crack?
Me: I don't know.
Isaac: It was the sun. The sun. It was ages ago.

Jan 14th 2010 He says, 'Mummy knows everything and Daddy knows a little bit.'

Jan 17th Fascination with his birth. He knows he was in Mummy's tummy and several times he says 'and then I popped out.' He asks how the tummy got closed up again.

Celia: With a needle, like sewing.
Isaac: Like knitting.

This fascinated him. Hours later he said to me 'if Mummy didn't want knitting her tummy would still be open – like a lift.'

Jan 21st Recent improvement. Whilst discussing which TV show he can watch before nursery he's given up saying 'when this finish' or 'after this one finish.' Now he says 'when this finishes.'

He uses 'yesterday' to mean any period in the recent past. A longer span is 'ages ago.'

This morning he looked for a stick from last night. 'Where can it be?'

He's started adding 'I think' to statements. And he gets particular about childish slang. If we say 'mahto' for tomato he says 'not mahto, tomato.' Same with 'ghetti.' He says 'not ghetti, spaghetti.' And he's stopped calling a cucumber a 'key-mama.' He's fussy about this. It's 'kew-cumber.' This morning he said that he'd had 'a bad dream.' I asked what happened and he said he 'was downstairs.' Usually – 'downladder.'

Me: Were there monsters?
Isaac: No.

He's never mentioned dreaming before. Sometimes he wakes up and says, 'I was thinking' and then relates a dream.

Jan 27th (aged 3 yrs, 7 months) He says 'luckily' for the first time.

Trouble constructing questions. Concerned about my transport method when I was little. I told him my mum didn't have a bike. He wants to know how I got around.

'Woss did she didn't have a bike?' ... ('why didn't she have a bike?')

He considered the reasons. 'Did she fall off? Did she have a accident?' He's keen to distinguish 'it was on purpose' from 'it was a accident.'

Getting a sense of time passing.

'That was a long time ago,' he says, asking if historical figures on TV are still alive or 'did he die a long time ago?'

Jan 30th 2010 I gave him some almonds. He ate two, then started peeling a third. 'Taking the paper off.' I encouraged him to eat the almonds.

Isaac: Is it nice for boys?
Me: Yes, it'll make you very strong.

Isaac: And biiiiiiig! Like you.

More peeling. I urged him to eat the almond rather than peeling it.

Isaac: When I don't take the paper off will it won't make me big?

Feb 10th Passing a memorial in Victoria park. 'That was a church a long time ago.'

The memorial looked like a ruined church, he thought.

Feb 11th Celia spotted a mouse (possibly a rat) in the kitchen. Isaac, upstairs, leaned down under the bed where Rita, the cat, lurked. 'Rita. There's a rat to catch.' He concedes that Rita's not good at catching rats, 'cos she's too old.' He thinks Rita might be dead or nearly dead. This comes out as 'is she bury?' Rita dies and her replacement is a kitten. Isaac calls it 'Kitten' thinking 'kitten' is a name and not the diminutive of 'cat.'

The name sticks – and years later Kitten becomes the world's oldest kitten.

Hearing a TV report about shootouts in Iraq.

Isaac: That man said 'firefight.'
Me: What's a firefight?
Isaac: It's when firemen have a fight.

Later.

Isaac: What's in my head?
Me: Not much.
Isaac: It's a brain. What's a brain look like?
Me: Cheese.
Isaac: It looks like a egg.

Feb 15th 2010 Playing 'at the doctor' with Isaac using his toy computer. Nine in the evening. Isaac interviews his patient (me).

Isaac: What's the problem?
Me: I dunno. What is the problem?
Isaac: You put a pen and a pencil and a pen in your eye. I just pretending.
Me: Oh.
Isaac: Did you always be dead in your house?
Me: No.
Isaac: Oh.
Me: Yes. I did.
Isaac: Good. What song did you want? Jingle Bells.
Me: OK.

Pause

Me: What was the problem again?
Isaac: You put a pen on your eye and just on your mouth and you throat it. Look on the screen ... This is close now. This is close. I have to go on my lunchbreak. I'm sorry, I have to go on my lunchbreak.

Minutes later, sitting on his big toy car.

Isaac: I'm going to my lunchbreak. I'm opening my, I'm opening my doctor, I'm just going on my lunchbreak. I will be back in a minute.

Pause

Isaac: I'm just having my lunchbreak, it won't take long, I've got cucumber and bread and butter.

[Ends]

His habitual explanation of death is 'dint have the right medsin.'

Feb 18th 2010 First sighting of 'that would be awful.'

Feb 27th (aged 2 yrs, 8 months) At a pub with a four-year-old who wolfs a big spoonful of Isaac's ice cream. The kid says 'my face hurts. I've got an ice cream head-ache.'

Pleading for a 'big warm' (milk), Isaac goes into a wheedling cycle: 'Get it, I need it, I want it, I need one, I need a big warm, I got to, I need a big warm, I got to, get it, get one, get a big warm, I need it, I want it, I got to.'

March 5th Returning from nursery, by bike, one day after meeting Marion.

Isaac: What's your family?
Me: You're my family.
Isaac: Uh?
Me: You're my family.
Isaac: Who's your dad after your mum?
Me: Uh? I don't know.

Pause.

Isaac: Who's my sister?
Me: You haven't got a sister.
Isaac: Is Marion my sister?
Me: No, she's my sister.
Isaac: She's a little bit my sister and a little bit your sister.

A request to use something now comes out as 'can we share?'

March 9th Celia watching *When Eight Bells Toll*. Isaac asks what it's about.

Celia: It's about helicopters and killing.
Isaac: I like helicopters and killing.

March 10th 2010 Asked about the Albert Memorial, Isaac suffers memory loss. I prompt him.

Me: The gold man with a gold face, remember?
Isaac: Did he didn't brush his teeth?

March 12th Isaac insists on taking a card to someone at nursery. Not sure who, probably a teacher. Later.

Me: Who did you give that card to?
Isaac: I don't know.
Me: What did she look like?
Isaac: She had a fat bottom. She had a fat bottom and she's called Gillian.

April 2nd 2010 (aged 3 yrs, 9 months) Confusion over past tenses.

'Did he went.'
'Did he saw.'

When celebrating a personal triumph, he says 'I winned' for 'I won.' Constant requests to be given TV-advertised toys 'on my birthday' (two months ahead)

April 6th Isaac sees me lick my plate.

Isaac: Don't lick your plate. Mummy doesn't lick her plate.
Me: She's a silly-billy.
Isaac: Don't say that!

A conversation about how long something might take. To check, he holds up three fingers on each hand, six in all.

Isaac: This minutes?
Me: Yes.
Isaac: That's not long minutes.

Drawing, he asks to be shown how to make a nine. I show him. He draws a nine. Celia and I go into ecstasies of congratulation. Then he adds a stalk lower down and says 'I made a flower.'

Returning after a car trip, he claims to have slept but 'I went to sleep with my eyes open.'

A game with buying & selling. He offers me a plastic car and I ask how much.

Isaac: That's one fifty.
Me: One fifty what?
Isaac: One fifty-nine.
Me: One fifty-nine quid?
Isaac: One fifty-nine quid, one fifty-nine pounds.

He finds an audio cassette, which he knows contains tape, so he wants to unspool it.

Me: You can't, it's special tape.
Isaac: Does it buy money?
Me: No.
Isaac: Does it measure things?
Me: It's music.

April 7th 2010 Going to the loo alone but wanting my proximity, for reassurance. I went with him half the way, promising to stay close, and he turned around. 'Are you serious?' (First sighting of that one)

He puts his hands behind his back, holding a toy in one hand, and asks me to guess which hand holds the toy. But he has as much fun revealing the truth as not. Hide and seek is equally flawed. His greatest joy is in revealing where he's hiding. Or he hides both hands behind his back and asks 'guess which is left, which is right.' He's convinced that this is a hard question.

April 13th First sighting of 'earlier' to mean 'some time earlier today.' Usually he says 'yesterday' to locate anything that happened in the past, whether half an hour ago, six hours ago, a week ago or a year ago.

'That's a great idea' rather than 'that's a good idea.'

First sighting of 'so' rather than 'very' or 'really, really' to intensify. He's starting to say 'so hard' rather than 'really, really hard.' I've only heard it twice. In moments of boredom, he looks up in vague entreaty and says 'whass I going do?' He's frustrated that his birthday is still months away. 'That takes ages, my birthday.'

Claire from the Museum of London is due to visit. His favourite museum is the Toy Museum.

Me: She works in a museum.
Isaac: Has she got toys?
Me: I don't think so.
Isaac: I think she has. How's she going to bring it?
Me: I don't think she's going to bring the museum.
Isaac: She going to bring it in a big big big big big big big BIG bag.

The days of the week are coming to him in a jumble. Whenever Celia and I ask each other for the time, we get an update from the sofa. 'It's seven o'clock. I think it is.'

Playing hide and seek in the park, he covered his eyes and counted fast to 20, missing out half the numbers after ten. He finished on '19, 20' and added 'eleventy, Thursday.' To indicate finality, he pronounced it 'eleventy Thurrrrrrsday.'

This morning, he's watering flowers with his water pistol. Water running low.

'I need more bullets, need get more bullets from the tap.'

Urged to do something – bath, teeth – he begs a reprieve so he can continue his current task and he holds up three fingers. 'After this minutes.'

He displays different arrangements of fingers and asks how many he's holding. I ask him to count them. This takes time and is always a voyage of discovery. He says 'one, two, three' as if these are wholly new and exciting concepts. He can barely count to four.

The pond. Watching tadpoles. I told him they'd turn into frogs. 'I want see make a frog.'

Me: It takes ages.
Isaac: Let's just wait.
Me: It takes longer than that.
Isaac: How many sleeps?

Returning through the park we passed a sleeping dog-walker.

Isaac: Whass happened to that man?
Me: He's asleep.
Isaac: He's dead.
Me: He's not dead. He's having a snooze.
Isaac: They killed him.
Me: No.
Isaac: Who kills people?
Me: Well, people who aren't very nice.
Isaac: Baddies. I want see someone kill someone.
Me: No, you don't.
Isaac: I want see someone die. Can I see someone die? I need see someone die.

Informed about the ash-cloud from the Icelandic volcano that grounded all aircraft, he explained the cause as 'the olvcano.' Given a gun by Celia, and aware that Grandma doesn't like guns, he set out with me to the park to do some shooting.

'Why Grandma doesn't like guns?'
'Because she's a pacifist.'
'I'm not a pacifist. I like killing.'

May 11th 2010 (aged 3 yrs, 10 months) We post a letter. He spots the letterbox. 'There's it.' He instantly corrects this to 'there it is.'

Asking questions about differences between a flat and a house. I tell him a flat is a house without a garden. Later we're watching David Cameron, on TV, on his way to Buckingham Palace to accept the premiership. He keeps pestering me to flip channels so he can watch *Sharkboy*. The change of government drags on. 'It takes ages' he says.

The car arrives at Buckingham Palace. Isaac gets interested. I try to keep him involved so he doesn't pester me constantly to flip to *Sharkboy*.

Me: He's gone to see the Queen. That's the palace where she lives.
Isaac: Is it a flat or a house?
Me: A house.
Isaac: Has it got a garden?

Then he asks about a hole which leads to queries about geology.

Isaac: What's a hole?
Me: A round thing, black, with nothing in it.
Isaac: What's a hole deep down, deep down there?
Me: Down in the centre of the earth?
Isaac: Yeah.
Me: It's fire down there, fire, to keep us warm.
Isaac: With a fire brigade?

He asked why our house wasn't on fire. He's getting his pronouns sorted out. This comes suddenly with no prompting:

Isaac: Him is a boy and her is a girl.
Me: That's right. What's 'he' and 'she'?

Pause

Isaac: She is a lady and he is a man.

He's become obsessed by No Smoking signs and wants to locate the No Smoking sign in cars, the bathroom, in buses. He's puzzled the house has none.

May 16th 2010 He returned from a trip to Suffolk, without me, which clearly involved a lot of directions while driving around. His new phrase is 'straight ahead.' I took him to see a dog-show, as it was closing, and he insisted there was another dog-show nearby 'straight ahead.'

In the bath, he said 'what's good luck called?' By 'called' he meant 'mean.' He defined good luck himself. 'It means have a nice, lovely day.'

Isaac to Leo, teaching him bad English. 'Daniella doesn't say no thank you, she says don't thank you.'

Isaac to Leo. 'My mummy's mummy died because they didn't have the right medsin.'

Leo, not to be outdone, 'my mum's dad died from a car. A car crashed on his back.'

Age **Four**

June in Spain, 2010 (aged 4 yrs, 0 months). He sees a facsimile of the Sphinx. 'It's a little bit lady and a little bit lion.'

Isaac: What's God look like?
Me: Like Grandpa but with a big white beard down to his knees.
Isaac: Can he fly?
Me: Yes.
Isaac: Why can he fly?
Me: So he can go anywhere and help people.
Isaac: Where does he live?
Me: In church. It's the house of God.
Isaac: No.
Me: Yes.
Isaac: It hasn't got a telly.

I collected Isaac from Leo's house. Leo's dad, Seskin, asked if I ever took Isaac to McDonalds – which I don't but I said 'I used to work at McDonalds.' Isaac heard this, made some deductions, and raised it during our bike-ride home. 'Why's McDonalds turned into the theatre?' I didn't get this until I realised: he knows I work in the theatre so he thought McDonalds had turned into the theatre. I said 'it hasn't turned into the theatre. I worked at McDonalds then at the theatre. They're different places.' Isaac unconvinced.

'Why's I can't see it turn into the theatre?'

Typical unanswerable question: 'Why's I'm not high up?'

Counting. He can get from one to ten. Then he goes ... '11, 12, 14, 18.' Then he gets confused. He's convinced there's a number 'eleventy' and he's very disappointed it doesn't exist. 'Why's there's not eleventy?' He goes through the tens between 10 and 100. 'Is there forty, is there sixty, is there seventy, is there eighty?' Oddly, he doesn't ask if there's 'three-ty' or 'five-ty.' He only asks about the ones that exist. He insists that 'eleventy' exists. Especially when he gets tired.

'There is eleventy. I know there is. There is eleventy in the numbers.'
'No there isn't,' I say.
'Draw it. Draw eleventy.'

Later, after thinking about numbers again, and practising counting, he said to me 'I'm worried about eleventy.'

He asks for translations into Spanish. How do you say 'television' and 'computer'?

He's puzzled how his birthday works. He was four on 23rd June. The next day, Koby told him he wasn't four. I asked why Koby said that. 'Because he said it wasn't my birthday.'

24th June 2010, the day after his birthday.

Isaac: Is I four today?
Me: Yes.
Isaac: Will I won't be four tomorrow?

He thinks he reverts to being three after his birthday.

Isaac: I didn't get much presents.
Me: Yes, you did.
Isaac: Ben Ten cards. A monster costume. And that's it.

Much puzzlement over past participles. He says ... gived, buyed, eatened, felled, broked, breaked, breakened, taked, catched.

July 2nd 2010

Isaac: Why is Gordon Brown not in charge any more?
Me: People didn't like him.

Isaac: Did you like him?
Me: No. Well, I did. He was a nice man but he wasn't good at being in charge.
Isaac: Who liked him?
Me: Not many people. Grandpa liked him.
Isaac: Did Nuala like him?

In the double-bed, in the morning. Isaac hides under the duvet. Celia and I pretend he's missing. We can't find him anywhere. We discuss where he might have gone, the shops, the beach, nursery. I pretend to call the police.

Me: Our little boy's missing. Can you find him please? He's wearing a Batman top, he's got blond hair and blue eyes, and he's four.
Isaac: (under the covers) Superman top!

July 10th – still worried about his age. 'Am I four today?'

Isaac: After four I come ten.
Me: No, five.
Isaac: After five I come ten.
Me: No.

After doing this all the way to nine, and doing some more counting, he says 'I'm worried about eleventy.'

Watching a Michael Jackson compilation video.

Isaac: Which one died?
Me: They all died. Well, no. There's only one. And he died.
Isaac: I want see him.
Me: You can't.
Isaac: Why did he die?
Me: Heart attack.
Isaac: Why?
Me: His heart stopped working.

Isaac: Why?
Me: He ate too much salt.
Isaac: Is I going have a heart attack?
Me: Not if you don't eat too much salt.

Later he asked about Michael Jackson. 'Did all of them die?' Michael Jackson starts singing *I am the Walrus* on my laptop.

Isaac: What's this about – what's he singing about?
Me: Walruses.
Isaac: What's walruses?
Me: Well, it's hard to explain. It's a Beatles song.
Isaac: Why's he singing about Beatles? Why's he singing about bugs?

A day later, after returning from the park, he asks 'why did Michael Jackson's mummy put too much salt in his food?'

July 11th 2010 Outside the Victoria pub, on top of a shed, we see a manikin of a man in a boat – an informal sculpture.

Isaac: Is he dead?
Me: No.
Isaac: Who made him dead?
Me: He isn't dead. Someone made him from plastic.
Isaac: Was that a long time ago in the 19th century?

(historical phrase comes from Celia)

August 9th (aged 4 yrs, 1 month) A nippy day. I collect Isaac from nursery.

Isaac: Can I have an ice cream?
Me: It's a bit too cold for ice cream.
Isaac: Cold likes ice cream.

Many questions and solutions.

Isaac: Why do builders wear hats?
Me: So that when a brick falls off a building it won't hurt their heads.
Isaac: They could bang it in with nails and it won't hurt their heads.

Aug 13th 2010

Isaac: Is Grandpa my great grand-dad?
Me: No. That's Jack Llewellyn Evans.
Isaac: Is he dead?
Me: Yes.
Isaac: I can get another one?
Me: No. How?
Isaac: Grow in Mummy's tummy.

He shows his Ben Ten costume to Celia but gets little reaction. 'I showed Mummy but she's not interesting.'

After Leo's holiday in Ireland.

Me: Has Leo got cousins there?
Isaac: He hasn't got cousins only old people.

Aug 27th (aged 4 yrs, 2 months) About to meet Celia's friend Tom, a teacher.

Isaac: What does he look like?
Me: Very nice.
Isaac: Does he tickle?

When he sees a photo of anyone, he asks 'is he dead?'
'Yes,' I say.
'Why did he die?
'Wrong medicine.'

I decided to change this answer. Isaac was singing his Michael Jackson favourite, 'may, may mekfeel,' a corruption of *The Way*

You Make Me Feel. He stopped and asked me a question for the millionth time. 'Why did Michael Jackson die?'

Me: His mum put too much salt in his food.
Isaac: Why?
Me: Actually, sometimes people just get old and die like that.
Isaac: Will I get old and die?
Me: What do you think?
Isaac: I think I will. 'May, may mekfeel.'

He was told that Auntie Sarah was going to babysit for him on a Monday evening. He rolled over and looked at me sheepishly. 'I'm not thinking about presents.'

A constant question: 'When I'm big will God make me not be naughty?'

Sept 3rd Cycling to Leo's, going over a big bump, I ask 'did you feel that bump?'

Isaac: Yes. Why do you don't know everything?

He refers to Seskin 'blowing cigarettes.' We've warned him about tobacco and he's an expert in the risks. 'They make your blood black and your heart doesn't work.'

He sings *The Farmer's Got A Wife* to himself.

Me: Do you want a wife?
Isaac: I don't need one. I've got Mummy.

When trying to evade things, he has a catalogue of excuses. 'I've got a headache. My tummy hurts. I'm ill. I am!'

Sept 12th 2010 Isaac starts school. Yesterday he put on his pyjamas and noticed a thread unraveling. 'It's unsewing.'

Looking for conkers.

Isaac: There's a conker tree.
Me: No, that's a plane tree.
Isaac: What's a plane tree?
Me: That.
Isaac: Why's it called a plane tree?
Me: I don't know. Perhaps because it's ugly.
Isaac: What?
Me: I don't know.
Isaac: What did you say?
Me: Nothing. It's a plane tree.
Isaac: Why's it called a plane tree?
Me: I don't know.
Isaac: Because, because it's a plane. Because it's, the leaves are like a plane. Why's it called a plane tree?

His desk is a footstool in the sitting-room. There he keeps his computer, some books, an old mouse, paper, pens and possibly a banana. His new exclamation is 'that might be a good idea.' He suggests working on his computer alongside me. 'That might be a good idea!'

Playing in the bath with flannels and cups, he says 'I'm doing a speriment.' When told of a forbidden action, like eating slug pellets or sticking metal rods into electric sockets, he always says 'will I die?' with an expectant look.

He spots canoes being unloaded on the canal. They're smaller than the barges.

Isaac: Why's they little?
Me: So just one person can use them.
Isaac: So they can have a bit peace and quiet – have a nap.

A typical question originates in a statement (usually trying out new vocab.) 'It's like a hula hoop. What's a hula hoop?'

Counting game. Isaac asks me to guess what number he's thinking of. 'I'm going give you a little clue. It begins with a wuh.'

Sept 22nd 2010 The bus was diverted to avoid a car crash. Isaac wants to see the crash. I explain the police cordon.

Me: So you can't go and look while they're tidying it up because the police put tape round it.
Isaac: They put Sellotape round it?
Me: Yes.
Isaac: So people don't get sweeped up.

Later
Isaac: What makes money?
Me: Work. You work and you get money.
Isaac: No, no, what makes coins?
Me: A special factory.
Isaac: I never had chocolate money for ages.

Sept 24th 2010 (Aged 4 yrs, 3 months) Isaac with a temperature. Home from school. Tucked up on the sofa in school uniform.

Me: You can have big warms today because you're sick.

[Isaac ponders as I go into kitchen to make big warms (milk). He appears in the hall]

Isaac: Sometimes when children are sick they buy a little present, don't they?

[back in the sitting room]

Isaac: Remember when my toe hurts, Mummy gave me a comic when my toe hurts. With Leo. And Leo got one too.

On the bus from school he asks questions, often prompted by the auto-announcement that names each stop.

Announcer: Lime House police station.
Isaac: Is it on this side or is it on that side? There might be a Lime House police station on this side and a Light House police station on that side. Noooo!

He asked why the police vans had lots of seats.

Me: So that baddies can sit down. Because when the police catch the baddies they need a rest. It's hard work being a baddie, bashing down doors, grabbing money, running away. And when they get caught they need a rest.

During this Isaac squirmed and complained loudly. He hated what I was saying, either for itself or for the implied mockery of him that it contained. He only calmed down when I assented to his suggestion that the baddies were held in a prison cell beneath the police van.

On the bus, discussing the name of the head-teacher, Miss Watt.

Isaac: Is that because she don't know nothing?

Oct 4th 2010

Me: Do you know what truth is?
Isaac: No.
Me: Do you know what a lie is?
Isaac: No.
[Pause]
Isaac: I do know actually.
Me: What's truth?
Isaac: When you know it is.

Oct 8th The park. Two adults riding a single bike. He asked its name. 'Tandem,' I said.

Isaac: Can I get a tanglem? You could get a tanglem and I can ride on the tanglem with you. That might be a good idea.

Oct 9th He notices, after 4 weeks at school, that his life has become different.

Isaac: Why does Leo doesn't come on Mondays?
Me: Because he has to go to school.
Isaac: Has it all changed, the world?

He dressed in a new outfit and showed it to Celia and me. 'Do I look cool?' he asked.

Then, a question we didn't grasp. 'Do I look like, with a hat, like a record-player?' He asked again. On 'hat' he mimed a baseball cap perched sideways on his head. And he mimed spinning discs with his index finger. So 'hat' is baseball cap and 'record-player' is DJ.

October 23rd (Aged 4 yrs, 4 months) Aberystwyth

Isaac: What's golf?
Me: When you hit a ball into a little hole.
Isaac: Can you get it out of the hole?

After hearing me on the phone asking for tickets to a 3.30 matinee, he asks, 'can you count up to 3.30?'

Watching TV in the morning. Ads start.

Isaac: Can have dis? Come here. Can have dis?

The ad is for toy mice.

Me: No. It's babyish. It's for girls.
Isaac: But I just like it. I want it.

A moment later, a mixing machine is advertised. He starts snapping his fingers to beckon me over.

Isaac: Can have dis? Dis. Dat.
Me: No, you've got mixing machines in the kitchen.

Constant questions which he's happy to answer himself. 'How do you make skin? You get paper and put bit of pink on and leave it to dry and that's it. How do you make eyes?'

And ... 'can metal bend? How can it bend?' Lots of questions about what's 'inside.'

'What's inside your tummy? What's inside bone? What's inside metal? What's inside the earth? What's inside your blood?'

Isaac, learning maths at school, sets me a problem. 'How many's this? Five.'

Nov 16th 2010 Bus. Isaac singing, 'the animals went in two by two.'

Isaac: Do you know that song?
Me: Yes.
Isaac: How do you know that song?
Me: I was four once.

[Amazement]

Isaac: Were you four?
Me: Yes.
Isaac: Were you one?
Me: Yes.
Isaac: Were you zero? [Pause] No, that would be a baby. How old are you now?
Me: You know. ... So, how old am I?
Isaac: A hundred.

Nov 19th 2010 Bus. He's talking about Shannon whose tooth has been removed. 'How do you take a tooth out?' I told him 'you have to pull very hard with a tweezers.' Which prompted a soliloquy. 'And then you get the tooth and you put the tooth under your pillow and then you go to sleep and that's it. Imagine if you took all your teeth out and then you could put them all under your pillow and you could get thousands of money.'

Nov 20th Bath-time.

Isaac: What happens if everyone dies?
Me: They aren't going to die.
Isaac: You don't know that.

Nov 21st Isaac cleans the fireplace on his own. He's praised and he concurs with the praise. 'I'm getting gooder at it because I'm getting bigger.'

Doing maths.

Me: What's one and one?
Isaac: Eleven.

Maths in the bath.

Isaac: What's 60 plus five?
Me: 65.
Isaac: Wait I'm goan trick you. What's five plus poo?
Me: I don't know.
Isaac: What's zero plus poo?
Me: Poo.

Isaac finds that hysterically funny. Later, hearing that Grandpa has had an operation and is in 'the room where you're nearly dead,' i.e. intensive care, Isaac says 'maybe they can give Cal Pol?'

November 27th 2010 (age 4 yrs 5 months) Card to Grandpa (my dad) dictated to me by Isaac. He recalls a step-ladder in the house.

Dear Grandpa,

We like you best.
I played on my step-ladder.
What do you want to do when you are better in our house?
Did it hurt when the doctors opened your tummy?
When you're better, can you dance?
No, you can't really dance because you're old.
My dad always works on his computer and he eats all the time.
I always like to dance.
Nuala is my best friend.
I want to write something all the way down to the end [of the card]
That's a great card.
[Signed]
Isaac

Singing carols on the bus.

'While shepherds watched their flocks by night/
Conceited on the ground.'

After starring as a Wise Man in a Nativity play at Temple Church.

Isaac: What's frank, frankin, what's frankset?
Me: Frankincense. It's a kind of fragrance to make the room smell nice.
Isaac: What's myrrh?
Me: Like baby oil. If baby Jesus needs a massage.
Isaac: Gold.
Me: That's money.
Isaac: Like chocolate money?

December 16th. Visiting a neighbour, David Muir, who worked for Gordon Brown. On the wall, a shot of David Muir with Gordon Brown. Close colleagues, clearly. I pick Isaac up to the level of the picture.

Me: Who's that?
Isaac: Gordon Brown.
Me: What does he do?
Isaac: He's in charge.
Me: Yes, he *was* in charge. Who's in charge now?
Isaac: David Cameron.
Me: And?
Isaac: Nick Clegg.

[David Muir was incredulous that Isaac knew this, aged four.]

December 17th 2010 Isaac plays I-Spy, indoors.

Isaac: I spy with my little eye something beginning with tuh, tyuh, chuh.
Me: Tuh or chuh?
Isaac: Tuh. Chuh. It's in here.
Me: Tree.
Isaac: Do you see a tree in here?
Me: No. Television?
Isaac: No.
Me: What does it begin with?
Isaac: Chuh. Tuh. I'll give you a little clue. It's yellow and it's got lines.
Me: Lightbulb?
Isaac: No.
Me: You're sure it's in here?
Isaac: It's outside.
Me: I thought you said it was in here.
Isaac: It's outside.
Me: Sun.
Isaac: No.
Me: You're sure it begins with a tuh. And it's outside.
Isaac: Yes.

Me: I give up. What is it?
Isaac: Bun.
Me: You said it began with a tuh. And you said it was outside.
Isaac: I changed the thing.

Isaac: Do you wish we had a big garden?
Me: No. Do you?
Isaac: I wish we had a big garden. Then I could play everywhere.

Isaac counting. He wants me to show him sums with my fingers. I'm reluctant. He's very tired. I want him to learn to count beyond 10 without counting all the way to 10 first on both hands.

Isaac: What's ten plus one?
Me: Eleven.
Isaac: Do the fingers.
Me: You don't need the fingers. What comes after ten? Eleven. So what's ten plus one? Eleven. Ten plus two? Twelve. Ten plus three? Thirteen. Ten plus four?
Isaac: Fourteen.
Me: Ten plus five?
Isaac: Fifteen.
Me: Ten plus six?
Isaac: You have to do the fingers.
Me: No. Ten plus six?
Isaac: I won't be your best friend if you don't do the fingers. I will kill you, with a chair, I will throw it at you, when I'm big if you're naughty.

Dec 30th 2010 (Aged 4 yrs, 6 months) Somerset. Isaac in the bath after washing up and cleaning parts of the grease-encrusted kitchen with Celia.

Isaac: This house is very dirty.
Me: Do you know who cleans it?

Isaac: Me and Mummy.
Me: No.
Isaac: Grandpa?
Me: No. He's not a cleaner. Ken and Jean clean it.
Isaac: In secret?
Me: No. They clean it every day.
Isaac: Why they don't want people to see them cleaning?
Me: Well, I'm not sure.
Isaac: Are they in a hurry?

Jan 1st 2011 Commenting on my bad knee which is slowly mending. 'When your foot really hurted you should had a bandage.'

Jan 10th Isaac watches *The Bourne Identity.* I tell him Jason Bourne is a special policeman and baddies are trying to kill him.

Isaac: Why's he not dressed as a policeman?
Me: He's hiding.
Isaac: I knows a good place to hide. Where there's a lot of poor people. [Pause] Africa? [Pause]. In a cupboard. [Pause]. In space. That's a good place to hide.

The film cuts to Paris.

Isaac: Is that the north pole?
Me: No, it's Paris.
Isaac: Is that *Disley* land Paris?
Me: *Disney* land Paris. No.

Jan 11th 2011 Me and Isaac watching Mr Tumble teaching sign language.

Isaac: What's the date today, not the day, the date?
Me: Eleventh of January.
Isaac: Leventh. This is how you sign 'forest.'

[He picks up some green chemical snot which he got from Violet]

Isaac: What's this made of?
Me: It's your snot.
Isaac: It's not snot. It's made.
Me: It's chemicals.
Isaac: It's yuk. It's smelly PlayDo. It's made.
Me: If you're good today, we'll go to the shop and get you a toy.
Isaac: Yes. I'll be very proud of you.

['Made' for 'manufactured.']

Jan 22nd Isaac in a bad mood. 'Just get out of this house!'

At the Science Museum, he asks 'what's science?' I tell him, 'clever things, tricky things.' He says, 'is this science?' He gets down on all fours and starts walking backwards down some shallow steps.

'Is that science?'
'No. Spaceships. That's science.'
'When you build steps to the moon and stick it on. Is that science?'
'Yup.'

[Referring perhaps to the steps of the Apollo 11 moon-lander]

Jan 23rd (Aged 4 yrs, 7 months) A tantrum before we go to the shop to buy a whistle. Finally Isaac agrees to leave. Sits in buggy looking cross. 'I'm just goan punch you in the face later.'

Leo and Isaac talk about Grandpa, (my dad, whom Leo knows.)

Leo: Ah, God love him.
Me: Why God love him?
Leo: He is so cute.
Isaac: He's sick.
Leo: Is Nuala sick?
Isaac: No, just Grandpa.

Leo: I know why he is sick. Because he's old. He's 81.
Isaac: How do you know?
Leo: Lloyd told me.
Me: He's older than that. He's 82. It was his birthday last week.
Leo: I'm older than him. I'm 86.
Isaac: No, you're not.
Leo: Yes. I'm 87.
Isaac: Let's just pretend we are eleven or twenty-one or six.
Leo: I'm 32.

Isaac looking through a magazine. 'Guess what, I found a good thing we could have if we moved a house and got a big garden.'

It was picture of a trampoline. A general observation, 1st February. 'I am the king of all this house.'

Feb 5th 2010 Difficult questions, part 18. 'When you talk does your skeleton talk?'

Isaac tells Leo about recent political developments. 'Gordon Brown was in charge but they didn't like him because he had one eye and a plastic eye like my mummy's dad.'

[Celia's dad has a glass eye]

Isaac puzzled by baldness. 'If things get cutted they grow again. And I think God gets tired at growing things because you have too much hair and he might make it again later. ...I just think of Grandpa, actually, that's why it comes of.'

Random questions

'Why does things break?

'Why are some things are soft and some things are hard? This is really interesting question. Shall I tell you it? I don't know why. Why are things, some things are soft and some things are hard?'

[I'm typing this on my laptop during bath-time. Isaac wants to help type]

Isaac: Can I see the page? I can't splash. But I can't type.

Isaac: Shall I tell you something really super-interesting question? How do you make spray? Can you give me a question and a answer?
Me: About what?
Isaac: About how do you make spray?

Random comment. 'You have to put some poisonous in it.'

Isaac: Have you been drinking champagne?
Me: No. Why?
Isaac: Cos it sounds like you are drunk.

I ask Isaac: 'How do you make black and white things?'

Isaac: You get some tiny weeny things which are squidgy and you dye it. Yeah? And it's done. And you put it in a machine and the machine makes it grow and you are done. Two machines you need, one if you want it small and one if you want it big.

March 2nd 2011 Reluctance to go to school with Celia. Ritual complaint. 'You are just a stupid Mummy.'

March 8th Watching a Hugh Grant romcom, *Nine Months*, where poor Hugh is abandoned by the girl. He's bereft.

Isaac: 'I've got a good idea. I've got a good idea how he can talk to her. He can write a letter.'

Sheer genius. Last year he was talking about teddy operations. Now he's a Hollywood script doctor.

March 10th 2011 Isaac and I come home from school. He confronts me in the kitchen. 'But I'm not a girl.' I ask for a repeat. 'But I'm not a girl.' He says it three times. 'But I'm not a girl.' Finally I realize that 'but' means 'good.' Or 'lucky that ...' He changes it.

'Good I'm not a girl.'

I ask why.

'Good I'm not a girl. When I grow up and I've got a baby in my tummy and they cut it out and it hurts. Good I'm not a girl.' He says he wants to marry Shannon.

I leave to see *Blithe Spirit* at the theatre and I tell him the story. 'About a man whose wife dies and he gets another wife and the wife who died comes back as a ghost.'

Isaac: Maths is going be tricky. [I'm not sure what this meant]

March 13th 2011 Leo watches the Japanese earthquake aftermath unfolding on TV in our house.

Leo: All the car and houses were throwing in the river. That happened in my house too.

Isaac thought this meant that Leo's car had been swept into a river by the Japanese earthquake but he didn't seem too concerned.

Isaac: We have to do our holy spirits.

A parody of church ceremonial done in all seriousness. Isaac picks up a letter and holds it like a hymnal and delivers a shouting chant.

Isaac: How do we do it! How would we do it! How do the holy spirits do it!

[He repeats this endlessly. No upward inflections to imply questions. I come in and parody him and he falls silent and hits my leg in an embarrassed way and then hits himself on the forehead three times, hard, and says, 'Ow!']

Isaac: You are a stupid Daddy.

[This shocks Leo]

Leo: He's not stupid.

Later, Isaac bounces on the bed with Leo. I'm next door.

Isaac: Hands up if you know which, what I'm singing. ... Hey it's tall buildings. Tidy up time. ...Listen. When I get angry my sharp claws come out.
Leo: It's 10.47.

Later

Leo: It's ten o'clock. Tidy up time.
Isaac: We are going to be learning about skeletons.
Leo: When it's quarter past we have go to lunch.
Isaac: Three-two-one. It's story time.
Leo: It's story time. Soon will be eleven.
Isaac: We are reading the pages. Pretend. Pretend there are words. I can't really read real so I'm gonna do it pretend. God love. There's one day, one day there was a dog called Parker. He was a really nice dog, one ear was up, one ear was down. One day Clarter cuddled his dog and put him on a little, he put some string on an old box and put wheels on the box and then made some string and put him on a lead and pulled him around.
Leo: Soon it will be lunchtime.
Isaac: And he drived him around and then he made it clean with soap and water and then they dried him out. And his brudder, he chewed toys, he loved chewing toys and his sister had seven teddies in her bed and she had slept with seven toys and then she fell out.
Leo: Nearly lunchtime.
Isaac: Lunchtime!
Leo: We will do more of this after lunch.
Isaac: Line up!

Leo: Please can you line up again please.
Isaac: We will do singing again in the office and then you will line up a bit later. I heard them shouting and being bossy. And I said 'Don't!'

Later

Isaac: Just line up. I'm not very pleased with you. No bath. No story. Just line up because we are very cross with you.
Leo: Don't. Don't even mention it. Jasmine and Sophie were being naughty and they go for Time Out when they come back from lunch. It's 10.19.

March 14th 2011 After a visit to Hill House – a potential new school – he comes back impressed by 'winning cups' (trophies). Later, as I change him after his bath.

Isaac: You going out tonight?
Me: No.
Isaac: Good.
Me: Oh, you like it when I stay in.
Isaac: Yes. I love you. And I like Mummy.

March 20th Victoria park

Isaac: Why's there not spice skating?
Me: Ice skating.
Isaac: Ice skating.
Me: Well, it's not cold any more.
Isaac: It's not winter enough.

March 22nd 2011 After Celia's latest outburst of loud, long and fruitless complaints about x, y or z. Isaac: 'Let's just pretend she is invisible.'

Morning. He comes into the sitting room and 'does work' at his desk. Quizzed about this he says, 'I'm doing my work. It's only boring work.'

25th March (Aged 4 years, 9 months) Isaac with me all day. Celia out. The next day, bath-time with Isaac. An almighty smash from the kitchen followed by sweeping up of glass.

Isaac: Mummy just broke something again.
Me: Does she break a lot of things?

[No reply, no denial either]

Isaac: I wish it was just you and me tonight. Why's that funny? Why are you laughing?

Bath-time. I take dictation on my laptop from Isaac. 'What, no actually why. Why did Gordon Brown, I mean David Cameron stop ... no actually start all over again. Why did David Cameron stop saying no actually, why did David Cameron stop, why did David Cameron wanted to be in charge instead of Gordon Brown. ... No I want to write a different one. Why did I go to the my new school? ... When I'm big ... what are you writing?'

'I'm writing what you say,' I said.

'He has, no when I get out of the bath,' said Isaac, 'can you tell me what to write and write it down. What you writed? What you writed? You writed I want to get out of the bath. Why. Why you writing that? No. I want to get out of the bath real. I want to get out of the bath real. Actually.'

[Later]

Isaac: When I get big I'm going to marry all the girls in the world. Not the ones that are already married.
Me: Who first?

Isaac: Mrs Dalton. I think she is already married.

[Mrs Dalton, South African teacher, 30]

April 2nd 2011 After hearing a story containing the word 'curious.'

Celia: Are you curious?
Isaac: I'm a lot curious about the Dust-Buster.

Leo and Isaac chat. They ask me for help periodically.

Leo: There is someone in heaven who disrespects God and he's very naughty. The Devil.
Isaac: Tears are your eye liquid.
Leo: Milk is liquid. Washing up liquid. Is washing up liquid, liquid?
Me: Yes.

Isaac points to some plastic bricks.

Isaac: God is actually in there. And if they want to pray to God they actually touch that.
Leo: Do you know God loves anyone even when they're naughty. Not really really naughty, just naughty. The Devil should live in prison.
Isaac: Why?
Leo: Because he's naughty. Do you know heaven is a really, really nice country. It's just inside the clouds and moon.
Isaac: Guess what's made up? The moon isn't made of cheese. It's just stone.
Leo: Do you know a place called Mars?
Isaac: No.
Leo: Mars is a kind of gas inside.
Isaac: This is not true. I said this, the moon isn't made of cheese and also there's no man in the moon.
Leo: But how about astronauts?

Isaac: The moon man is actually on the moon but he has a body actually.
Leo: Do you know what an astronaut is?
Isaac: No.
Leo: They eat dry food.
Isaac: They eat the moon.
Leo: Yeah, they eat the moon.

Leo's Turkish father, Seskin, arrives and discusses Una's new baby (Leo's cousin.)

Me: What's the baby called?
Seskin: You know, I not good with this. Leo. What's Una baby name?
Me: Leo, what's Una's baby called?
Leo: Elizabeth Grace. That's a very long name. That's two names.

Isaac on the origin of wee. 'The orange juice goes down the tummy through your tummy and then it goes into the ball and there's a little round window and the ball makes the orange juice and then the door and the ball slides the door open and then the wee comes out on the bone and slides down the bone and then it comes out of your willy.' [Pronounced 'woolly']

Isaac gives random dictation. 'God made a country, he drawed on some paper and then he did magic and then it came to live and that's it. There. That's it. Can you read what I just said?'

Isaac dictates. 'Does the water from the bath go through the plug and then through the tube and then into the sea and then it goes into a big, big, um, into a big, um, river and then it goes into a stream and then it goes into a little pond, a pond, and then through into a pipe and then out of a tap.'

Me: Who told you that?
Isaac: I just thought about it.

April 7th 2011 Isaac dictates during bath-time. But I don't have my laptop.

Isaac: Write what I say on your computer.
Me: No, I can't.
Isaac: Please. Please write. Just one minute. One minute is not long.
Me: OK.

[I get the laptop]

Isaac: OK. Let's do a story. OK. What you writing? OK. Now we are reading a book about the, a tree and a fox. Now once upon a time there was a fox. Not just a fox, a magic fox, he had golden eyes, he was called Bolt. No, no, no. Just cross that out. Delate all that. Delate what I just said.
Me: It's gone.
Isaac: Good. This story is about Bolt. One day there was a dog called Bolt. He was a puppy. And then he came big and then he went in a special machine and he was a super-dog. And he had an owner. And then he was, he met a cat and a hamster and then he just, no he swinged on a sign and then they jumped onto a train and then they jumped onto the roof. And then they got up and they fell off and they went onto the track and then ... the end. No not the end. And then the hamster had superpowers. The end. The dinosaurs and the pants. The dinosaurs and the pants. And the spray.

[End of story]

Home from school. Isaac lolling on sofa. Me with him. Celia in kitchen.

Isaac: Ice cream is good for boys.
Me: Yes, well I'm not giving you ice cream. You're going to have supper.

[Isaac toddles into the kitchen with a new ploy]

Isaac: Mummy. Ice cream is good for bad tummies.

May 3rd Isaac, up at 7 am, awakens Celia with a demand. 'If Shannon's mum and dad are busy she can come here. Phone them. Phone them now!'

May 22nd Leo reacts to Celia's huge spread for lunch. 'You're a beautiful cooker.'

Isaac was being taken home by Ishan's parents on the train. Ishan took a spare seat next to an old lady. Isaac approached the old lady and told her to give him her seat. Later we told Isaac about this.

Us: You can't ask an old lady to move. She's more important than you.
Isaac: I'm more important than her because I've got more stuff, I've got more work stuff.

['Work stuff' means computers, papers and phones which he plays with in the morning]

May 23rd (Age 4 yrs, 11 months) Isaac interviews Rita, the ageing cat. He pushes the microphone at her snout.

Isaac: What's one plus six?
[Rita makes a plaintive bleat. 'Miaow.']
Isaac: Is it miaow? Is that the answer? What's four plus four?

Isaac leaves for school. I promise him that I'll help 'make things' later. Last week we made a boat.

Isaac: We can make a house. Or a sea. We can make a whole country.

In bath.

Isaac: How do paper aeroplanes fly?

Me: They sort of float. Wave your hands, you can feel the air, it's like a sort of sea and they float on it.
Isaac: I think that's a question for Isaac Newton. Why do people take my names? A girl at school took my wish.
Me: How many wishes did you get?
Isaac: One.
Me: And what did you wish for?
Isaac: I want to be a singer when I'm a teenager ...

Later

Isaac: Tell me other people who are in books.
Me: Napoleon.
Isaac: Who's he?
Me: A super soldier.
Isaac: Like me. When did he die?
Me: In 1821, I think.
Isaac: Is that the fir were war?
Me: First world war. Or second world war?

Isaac giggles at these names.

Isaac: Who won?
Me: Who won the second world war?
Isaac: Yeah.
Me: Britain, America and Russia.
Isaac: [disappointed] Ohhhh.
Me: What?
Isaac: I want England to win.

Isaac opens a shop and writes a two-sided sign – 'oapin' and 'cloost.'

May 29th 2011 Isaac's story.

Isaac: Once upon a time, no don't write once upon a time don't write it, don't type that. The story is called, there was an old lady who swallowed a fly.
Me: You've already said that.
Isaac: No, you have to say it again. There was an old lady who swallowed a different animal. I don't know why she swallowed a spider to catch the fly. Take all of that away, what I just said. Are you writing what I just said? Don't. Just.... Can I just see what you have wrote? Tell me what you have written. Tell me what you have written down. Daddy. Daddy! Tell me what you have wroten down. Daddy! Daddy, are you typing? Cancel all of that. Just cancel all of that.

May 31st On the way to Leo's, he asks why concrete is hard.

Me: I don't know. It's full of things that make it hard.
Isaac: Why is there no concrete in space?
Me: People haven't built anything in space.
Isaac: What's inside the sun?
Me: Hydrogen.
Isaac: What's hydrogen?
Me: Fuel. Like petrol.
Isaac: What colour is it – what colour is petrol?
Me: Er, black. Sort of.
Isaac: What happens if you drink it?
Me: You die.
Isaac: Is it poisonous?
Me: Very.
Isaac: I know what a poisonous mushroom looks like, red with white spots. And I know a toad is a big frog.

In a book Isaac finds a picture of Isaac Newton whom he recognises. He asks me to point out the word 'Isaac' even though he can read it.
Isaac: Where does it say Isaac?

Me: There. Are you going to be as clever as Isaac Newton when you grow up?
Isaac: I am Isaac Newton but I'm still a child.

Isaac always wants to know if I'm going out. He usually asks, late afternoon.

Isaac: You goan out tonight?
Me: No.
Isaac: Yayyyyy!

This morning, he's in bed with diarrhea which has lasted a week. He's groaning but he stops when I come into the bedroom. He wants to know if I'm writing a political sketch. It's Tuesday. So, no.

Me: Come and watch Beebies.
Isaac: I'm just goan tell you something. Have you got to watch the news & type about it?
Me: Not today.
Isaac: Yayyyyy.
Me: But I've got to work though.
Isaac: Thass OK.

Age **Five**

June 23rd 20011 Isaac's birthday. On the bus. 'If you put a zuh at the end of a word, that means there are more. Like ice cream zuhhh. Ice cream is a funny word because there's a scream in it.'

Later

Isaac: Why aren't you allowed to talk to strangers?
Me: Because they might not be nice.
Isaac: They might be baddies.
Me: Yup.
Isaac: I talked to a stranger.
Me: When?
Isaac: A long time ago. Have you talked to a stranger?
Me: Yes.
Isaac: What did he look like?
Me: I've talked to lots of strangers.
Isaac: Was it a boy or a girl?
Me: I've talked to lots of strangers. It's OK if you're an adult.

Many questions about the 'stranger' I once daringly talked to. Eventually, on the sofa after a nice birthday, Isaac looks at me.

Isaac: I'll be sad when you die.
Me: Thanks mate.

Learning to read. He reads 'paint' easily. Then he sees a similar word in a kids' book.

Isaac: What's gaint? [giant]

Getting very stroppy and tired in the evening. 'I'm not your friend any more. I won't ever be your friend.'

July 5th Celia and I refused to buy him an ice drink from the shop. 'I want you to go in the garden. Both of you. I want you both to go in the garden.' Banishment from the house! Much kerfuffle over his bath. In the bedroom I put on his pyjamas.

Isaac: I want to just throw you out of the window.

July 8th 2011 Isaac and Shannon.

Isaac: I need to go to the loo.
Shannon: Can I watch you?

[Later]

Isaac: Come in my room. We can hide.
Shannon: What's this?
Isaac: I'll get my lip balm.
Shannon: Where's your lip balm?
Isaac: I'll get my lip balm.

On TV they watch the NASA space shuttle about to blast off.

Shannon: My Daddy is watching this. Or the cricket. I'll have to tell him if he's watching science or cricket.

The final Shuttle launch ever. Isaac knows this in advance. Shannon's parents have a car and they refer to petrol as 'gas.' Isaac doesn't know that 'gas' means petrol. And Shannon has never heard of petrol. She says 'gas' or 'gas-oil.'

Me: This is the last one. They've run out of money.
Shannon: They can get some more money and blast-off another rocket.

After blast-off they run around playing an energy gathering game.

Shannon: We have too much gas. The gas is running out. We have one hundred and fifty-nine of gas.

Isaac: Take the plug out – so none comes in.
Shannon: Four-three-two. Blast-off again. Quick. The baddies are coming again.
Isaac: I got there. Ok. I have to put some petrol again.
Shannon: Remember the gas-oil.
Isaac: This is nine percent. This is the petrol I have to put in. Nine percent. Sixty. Sixty hundred. Sixty hundred million thousand!
Shannon: We have a gas-shop in the rocket. We should, we use it all. Put it in.
Isaac: There, I got it all.
Shannon: Mm.

Isaac runs up to me with a heavily threaded curtain cord.

Isaac: Daddy. Can you undo this knot?
Me: What for?
Shannon: It's part of our game. It's our anchor.

Knot impossible to untangle.

Me: Sorry. That's the best I can do.

Off they run.

Shannon: Quick get the bullets. Get the bullets out. This is our bullet gun.
Isaac: This is their bullet. Beeep. Beeep. Pwchh!
Shannon: Is this how you shoot the bullets?

Shannon is great fun. Her parents move to Dubai and Isaac never sees her again.

July 17th Isaac's random chat. 'I like all the colours, except pink. And black. Do you like all the colours except pink and black? I like the light, bright colours but not the dark colours.'

Isaac with Celia, vaguely, in the background.

Isaac: Fire cannon, now. Fire cannon now, I said. We have to fire a cannon now. A real cannon. How much are cannons? How much are pirate ships? Are they ten ninety hundred? They have wee on the floor.
Celia: Who?
Isaac: Pirates. They don't have toilets. ... One day there was a big, big sword but no ship.

At Brockwell Park. My brother and Georgina are selling food from a stall. We help for 20 minutes. It's not busy. He said, 'I didn't help much because I had to have lots of breaks. And I gave you your cake.'

The bus home from school.

Isaac: What's dee sable mean?
Me: Disabled. It means you've got an arm missing or a leg that doesn't work or you can't see.
Isaac: And you're not allowed to laugh at them.

July 20th 2011

Isaac: I don't know who I'm going to marry yet.
Me: Shannon?
Isaac: No
Me: Mrs Dalton?
Isaac: She's already married.
Me: Nat?
Isaac: He's a boy.
Me: Doesn't matter. You can marry a boy.
Isaac: OK, I'll marry Nat. Are you joking?
Me: No, you can marry anyone. You can marry a dog. Or a wasp.
Isaac: It would always sting you.
Me: You could marry a car. But it would *drive* you mad.

[Joke fails]

July 21st On the bus to Nat and Ezra's.

Isaac: Why are some people not married?
Me: Don't want to. Prefer to be alone. Which is better?
Isaac: Married. Then you have friends and a little child. ... Little children are good.
Me: [looking pointedly at him] Some are bad!
Isaac: I'm not that bad.

Unanswerable question Number Gazillion.

Isaac: When's next week?
Me: Well, it's next week.
Isaac: I don't understand.
Me: Well, I don't understand the question.
Isaac: When is it? Tell me. When is it?

'Next week' never arrives as 'this weekend' arrives or 'the end of term' or 'Christmas.' Of course! Future events occur and then move into the past but 'next week' is a reference point not an event. We never wake up and say, 'at last, it's next week.'

Learning to read. Isaac spelled 'HE' for the first time, letter by letter.

'H' is 'huh' and 'E' is 'air.'

Isaac put them together and said 'huh – air' & assumed that 'HE' was pronounced 'hair.'

Seeing RBS, or Royal Bank of Scotland, he said 'ruh buh suh.' Robbers. Which is about right.

July 22nd He's on my shoulders coming back from Nat and Ezra's and I can't see where he's looking. He spells out a road sign painted on the Tarmac. 'Wuh – uh – luh – suh. WALLS.'

Me: Good, Isaac. Where do you see that?
Isaac: There.
Me: Where?
Isaac: There.

I can't see it. We continue along the pavement. He spells it again. 'Wuh– uh – luh – suh. WALLS.'

Me: Where does it say WALLS?
Isaac: There.
Me: Where?

I see SLOW painted on the road. He read it backwards. WOLS. To him it doesn't matter.

Me: That's 'SLOW.'
Isaac: Why's it say 'SLOW'?
Me: So cars slow down and don't bash each other.

Friday July 23rd 2011

Isaac: Is glun a word?
Me: Glun? No.
Isaac: What's a word?

Meaning 'give me another word.'

Me: Revolution.
Isaac: Rib ooshun. What's rib ooshun?
Me: When there's a war to see who's in charge.

July 26th 2011 (Age 5 yrs, 1 month) Isaac dressed as a surgeon, complete with green hat, explaining his medical costume to Leo. 'You know why doctors wear these hats. Because if they're opening a tummy, pieces of hair go in the tummy.'

July 28th Isaac and Leo.

Isaac: Where does water come from?
Leo: Ice.
Isaac: Hills.

Me, trying to put Leo's shoes on while he's entranced by a TV show. I want him to put his own shoes on.

Me: Can you put your shoes on yet? Leo? Can you put your shoes on yet? Leo? Can you put your shoes on yourself?

Leo looks at me evenly.

Leo: You're getting quite old aren't you.

Later, Leo is frustrated at Isaac's refusal to go out.

Leo: He's not the boss of this house.

Later.

Leo: I think you've got a good house but not a good son.

Isaac's unanswerable question Number 2 million. 'What happens if a bit of food gets stuck in your heart?'

For a few months he's been saying 'newsed' instead of 'used.' So he says, 'Mummy newsed to smoke.' He says 'I newsed to do this' and 'I newsed to do that.' I correct him occasionally but it makes little difference.

August 5th 2011

Isaac: When was I born?
Me: On your birthday. When's that?
Isaac: 23rd. Of June. When's your birthday?
Me: Sixth of March.
Isaac: You're before me. I've got a bigger number than you.

Naming a large number he said 'one hundred thousand million' for the first time getting the order correct. Usually he jumbles it all up. 'One million thousand hundred and sixty.' In recent months he's asked to 'do a experiment.' This involves placing bowls on the sitting-room floor and making a mixture of flour, sugar, tea and water. And he likes putting a biscuit in a see-through plastic bag and bashing it into crumbs. The ingredients, mixed together with a spoon, have to go into the oven overnight. Next day, after being removed from the oven, that's it. He's no longer interested. Leo likes doing the experiment too.

22nd August 2011 I said to Leo and Isaac, 'after I've finished work we're going to the Tower of London.'

No response from Leo. Possibly because I've never mentioned the Tower of London to him.

Me: Do you like the Tower of London?
Leo: Yeah of course. I love the Tower of London. You know I do.

Isaac's mad logical universe. He comes downstairs dressed in a skeleton costume wearing swimming goggles and holding a strip of clear plastic paper which he wants to cut. 'Daddy. Can I have scissors?'
Me: OK. What are you doing?
Isaac Playing hospitals [which he states as if it's obvious]
Me: Who's ill?
Isaac: My giraffe.

Unanswerable question number gazillion. 'How many lights are there in the world?'

Me: I don't know.
Isaac: Three million.

Aug 26th 2011 (Aged 5 yrs, 2 months)

Isaac: What happens if a child smokes a cigarette?

Truthful answer 'nothing.' For predictable reasons I lie.

Me: Their lungs go black and they get ill and die.

I make popcorn on the stove. When it starts popping Isaac jumps on a chair and shouts 'popcorn world' and runs around picking up the popcorn and scoffing it. He even clears up afterwards with the Dust-Buster. Later we visit the park after rainstorms. Slugs crawling everywhere. Isaac yells 'it's slug world!'

Isaac and Leo open the First Aid box. Leo reads the tubes and packs. Isaac is sent to me to interpret.

Isaac: What's anti seppic?
Me: Kills germs.

After I interviewed Tara Fitzgerald, she pops up on TV. 'See her?' I said. 'I met her yesterday.'
Isaac: So she's true.

Aug 27th 2011 Isaac considers the spelling of 'bird.' He thinks it should be spelled with two letters, b and d. That's all. 'BD.'

Isaac: It's buh, duh. Bird. How's it really spelled?
Me: Bee eye are dee. It used to be 'brid.' Bee are eye dee.
Isaac: Did you say 'brid' when you were little?
Me: I'm not that old, I mean 600 years ago.

Me at home. Isaac and Celia on the train to Somerset. I telephone them and I'm handed over to Isaac. No introduction – straight into the questions.

Isaac: What colour is water?
Me: It doesn't have a colour. You can see through it.
Isaac: It's white, a special kind of white.

Me: Are you on the train?
Isaac: It's going.
Me: Good.
Isaac: Why do they don't have seatbelts on trains?
Me: Ask Mummy.

[Pause]

Isaac: They don't need them. Because they don't stop fast like ... (makes a screeching noise). They don't stop like .... (more screeching noises).

Recent mispronunciations. 'Venchtable' for vegetable and 'Dr Who Confinential' for 'confidential.' Unanswerable question Number 10 billion:

Isaac: What am I going to say?
Me: I don't know.
Isaac: Guess.

The pond. He fills a small plastic bag with water and swings it around. I try to get him to come home and he agrees immediately. As long as he can take the bag of water. I set off. He lags behind me with his bag of water.

Isaac: This is bed-time water. What is bed-time water?
Me: You just invented it.
Isaac: What?
Me: You invented it.
Isaac: I can't hear you. What is bed-time water?
Me: You invented it.
Isaac: But what is it? What is bed-time water?
Me: You tell me.
Isaac: What is it?
Me: You called it that.
Isaac: What is it? Tell me. Pleeeeese!

Later I realise that 'bed-time water' is given to Imogen, his friend, at bed-time. A hot water bottle.

Leo arrives on the eve of Isaac's first day back at school in September. Celia explains, 'we're not doing fun things today. We have to get Isaac ready for school. So it's shops, not fun things. Is that OK?'

Leo: Well, I don't think so, no.

Celia leaves the house alone. Later.

Isaac: Where's mummy gone?
Me: Doctor.
Isaac: Why?
Me: Get a pill to help sleep.
Isaac: Will she sleep at the doctor?

Unanswerable question, number 4 million.

Isaac: How big is an ant's brain?
Me: Teeny.
Isaac: How big is an ant's skull?
Me: Teeny weeny.
Isaac: Can you see it?
Me: Just about.

Sept 22nd 2011 Isaac wakes up early, singing, 'I like to move it, move it. I like to move it, move it.' He asks Celia. 'What does *I like to move it, move it* mean?'

Sept 23rd 2011 (Aged 5 yrs, 3 months) The park. After inventing exercise routines, running up and down the path, Isaac is worried his heart is beating too fast. It's dark, 8pm. Perhaps he needs the hospital.

Isaac: Is it still open?
Me: It's always open.

Isaac: But they might get tired.

This concerns him a lot but now he understands.

Isaac: In the morning the night-time people rest and in the night-time the morning time people rest.

Then, from nowhere ...

Isaac: Are girls better than boys or are boys better than girls?
Me: What do you think?
Isaac: Boys *and* girls.

Looking at a 'bone book' from school, he says the tibia and fibula resemble a violin bow. He's about to go to bed in Celia's room. I asked him when he'll start sleeping alone. 'When I'm sixty ten. That's not even a number.'

A phone call with Grandma. Isaac is told he's going to get a present. But the only info she gives is that it's red, green & bouncy. After the phone call, he tries guessing. 'A trampoline, a football, a pogo stick?' All wrong. He settles back and folds his arms. 'Let me think.'

He keeps reviewing his guesses.

'When I said it was going to be a trampoline was that a good guess?'

He thinks I know what the present is. I don't. In fact it's a kite. Which I hide so he never gets it. I hate flying kites.

Watching Liverpool v Newcastle. A Newcastle striker boots the ball into the crowd.

Isaac: How many points is that? It went into the people. That's six points.
Me: No, you're thinking of cricket. They have to get it in the goal.
Isaac: Oh yeah. I forgot.

He thinks there are three teams. One in blue, one in black and one in red (the referee.) Liverpool's Luis Suarez is substituted.

Isaac: Why's he got to watch?

Making comparisons with rugby.

Isaac: Why do they get hurt in rugby?
Me: That's the rule. They're allowed to bash each other.
Isaac: They shouldn't had made that rule. I'm never going to play rugby ever.

In the park cycling on his bike, minus the stabilisers, which he calls 'staplers.'

Me: I'll be really proud of you if you can ride the bike.

He wobbles along for 10 seconds and peters out in some lumpy grass. But he did OK. I was impressed.

Isaac: Daddy, are you proud with me?

He's keen to throw the 'staplers' away or to sell them. The next day, when we practise again, he wants the staplers re-attached.

September 27th 2011 With Celia, watching a film, *Volcano*. Everyone's escaping from disaster.

Celia: I think I'd get into a car and drive away.
Isaac: I think I'd move house. Really fast.

Unanswerable question number 4,602. Sept 28th

Isaac: How bossy is your brain?
Me: Not very.

Isaac points around his body.

Isaac: No. It tells every bits of your body to do.

Trying to explain electricity and gravity. He knows electricity was 'invented' by Michael Faraday and that Isaac Newton observed gravity. 'Why's he called Isaac?' This puzzles him a lot. We were watching a show about 17th century homes and he seemed outraged that they didn't have lights. I told him they didn't have electricity back then. 'Did they have gravity?' He assumes that gravity, like electricity, is a recent development.

Isaac: Do they have gravity in space?
Me: Yes.
Isaac: No, they don't!
Me: Oh no, because people float around, don't they.

He always wants to know if things are 'true' (real) or not.

Isaac: Are poison arrow toads true?
Me: No.
Isaac: Poison toads?
Me: Yes.
Isaac: What colour are they?
Me: Green.
Isaac: Are witches true?

I was inclined to deny this but Celia chipped in.

Celia: Yes.
Isaac: Bad witches?
Celia: Yes, bad witches and good witches.

This got Isaac thinking.

Isaac: Does God kill bad people?
Me: Yes.
Isaac: How?
Me: Thunderbolts. He throws lightening at them.
Isaac: I hope he throws lightening at bad witches.

Oct 5th 2011 Unanswerable question on bus. 'How much places is there?' Meaning how many countries/continents exist. He counts them. (Africa features a lot because Mrs Dalton is from South Africa.)

Isaac: Africa, Australia, India, South Africa, America.
Me: You had Africa twice.
Isaac: Oh yeah. Africa, Australia, South Africa, India, New Zealand.

He runs out of continents/countries.

Me: What about where we are?
Isaac: Oh yeah. London.
Me: What about where Marion lives?
Isaac: Wales. That's in London.
Me: No, it's not.
Isaac: Wales.
Me: What about where Grandma comes from?
Isaac: Wales.
Me: That's where she lives. Not where she comes from.
[Isaac is blank]
Me: Grandma comes from where Leo's mum comes from.
Isaac: Ireland.
Me: Yes. And Leo's Dad?
Isaac: Turkey. I think that's ten.

Oct 8th With Celia, we pass a hobbling drug-addict stumbling around the park.

Isaac: Is he drunk?
Celia: He's been taking drugs.
Isaac: Does that mean he's taken them from someone's suitcase?

Referring to a TV show about customs searches at airports.

Isaac and me. Isaac has a solution to the problem of existence.

Isaac: What if there was no world, no God, no colours, nothing. Then it would all be?
Me: Non-existent.
Isaac: See through.

Isaac is hooked on quizzes.

Me: What do you want for your lunch tomorrow?
Isaac: Guess.

Later

Isaac: You're not allowed to say Boo at my school. You're never allowed to say Boo. Except in a pantomime. That's what pantomimes are for. Saying Boo.

October 15th 2011 We want to buy a bicycle horn for Leo's birthday. No bicycle horns are available so Isaac pesters me to buy something else – for him – anything, at a toyshop on Roman Road. I refuse. He complains bitterly as we go home and says I indulge myself with purchases. 'You always buy things.'

Me: No, I don't. I just buy food. Anyway I'm a grown up.
Isaac: When I'm a grown up I'm still going to have lots of toys. And play with them. And buy them. Always, always, always, always, ALWAYS.

Which turns into a lengthy song about 'always always always.'

Oct 29th Isaac looking at a children's encyclopedia. 'Are these very learn-about?'

Isaac on synonyms.

Isaac: There's two Bs. B in the alphabet and bee that makes honey.
Me: There are three. There's 'be' as in 'be quiet.'

Isaac: There's four Bs. B the noise a bee makes. Buzz.
Me: That's buzz not B.
Isaac: How do you spell buzz?
Me: Buh, uh, zuh, zuh.

Bonfire night, **Nov 5th 2011**. Isaac desperate to leave the house. Me searching for lost keys. 'Can you don't be a slowcoach cos it's nearly the time.'

More unanswerable questions.

'How much colours is there?'
'How much trains in London?'
'How much lines in London?' (tube lines)

Nov 8th 2011 Isaac in the bath, asks how you 'make butterflies.'

Me: They come from caterpillars.
Isaac: How?
Me: In the spring.
Isaac: When's spring?
Me: Do you know what it is now?
Isaac: Autumn.
Me: Then?
Isaac: Winter.
Me: Then?
Isaac: Summer. No, Spring. January February, March, April, May, June, July, September, November, October, November, December. Is the world going to end?
Me: Don't think so.
Isaac: My mum says the world's going to end.
Me: When?
Isaac: Don't know.

Nov 15th The bus home. Isaac boasts about eating his lunch which I'd made him. He'd eaten less than he claimed.

Isaac: I ate all my sandwiches.
Me: Even the crusts.
Isaac: Not the crusts. I don't like crusts. They don't make you strong.
Me: They do. Only girls don't eat crusts. That's why girls are weak.

He's momentarily dazzled by 'weak' – a new word. Awe-struck, he makes a connection.

Isaac: Superman is weak when they put kryptonite.
Me: Yes.
Isaac: Maybe there's a girl in kryptonite.

At this I laughed so loudly that he continued the conversation with his hands over his ears.

Nov 17th 2011 Early, Celia trying to get him to school.

Celia: We're so late.
Isaac: Will they tell off you?

Ancient History with Isaac – who turns out to be politically correct.

Isaac: Who were the Begyptians?
Me: The Egyptians.
Isaac: When were they?
Me: Before the Romans.
Isaac: Begyptians and then?
Me: Then the Greeks.
Isaac: And then?
Me: The Romans.
Isaac: And then?
Me: Well, the Romans lost their empire so there were lots of wars.
Isaac: What's empire?

Me: When you go to someone else's country and say this is my country.
Isaac: I think if you do that you'd go to jail.

Isaac learning about Grandma's hip replacement.

Isaac: They could get a leg from a dog and give it to her. Or a dinosaur.

Dec 16th Science Museum. Looking at models of ships. Isaac's questions are 'is it a warship?' and 'did it sink down?' He refuses to walk anywhere and offers a litany of excuses. 'I'm too tired, my leg hurts, I've got tummy ache,' etc.

Afterwards.

Me: Was it a nice day? OK? Or a bit boring?
Isaac: A very, very nice day.

Dec 17th Isaac says he wants to go to bed at nine o'clock. Feeling tired at 8.40. 'How much minutes to nine o'clock?'

He sees me reading a book subtitled 'Summary of Present Thinking.' He spells out 'Summar' so I complete it for him, 'Summary.'

Isaac: Is this book all about Summary?
Me: No.
Isaac: What page is it?
Me: Look and tell me.

I'm on p 308.

Isaac: Thirty hundred eighty.
Me: Three hundred and eight.

Watching *Harry Potter*, he asks if it's real or 'are they actors?' I say it's not real. 'Is it non-fiction?' he asks. Later, during a sequence involving spells and wands ...

Isaac: How do wands work?
Me: Don't know.
Isaac: You know the wands, when people are dressed up as magicians and people and when you hold their wands you know they actually break, you know those kind of wands?
Me: No.
Isaac: The wands that break. The wands that break. Silly people have wands that aren't really wands. They're just wands with string in the middle and when you hold it, it breaks.
Me: Yeah. Magicians.

A morning argument over a broken plastic milk bottle. Celia goes to the shops. Isaac needs a new bottle but he's worried he won't get it. 'Maybe Mummy won't buy me a bottle because I didn't be nice to her.'
Me: Did you hit her?
Isaac: No.
Me: She said you hit her.
Isaac: With what?
Me: Your hand.
Isaac: Not very hard. Like this ... [strikes the chair arm lightly]

Restaurant with Isaac in South Kensington. I tell him we have to avoid the rush hour. 'When everyone wants to get home in a hurry.' He's fascinated. He likes the concept of the deadline but he doesn't take to the term 'rush hour' as I'd expected.

Isaac: How much minutes is it?
Me: Till what?
Isaac: The busy thing.

Dec 22nd 2011 Tomorrow Isaac will be five and a half. Holes appearing in the Santa myth.

Isaac: Why is there always Santa dressed up?
Me: Because people want to see him.
Isaac: Why can real Santa not come?
Me: He's busy.

I half hoped he'd ask searching questions about appearance and reality, about particulars and universals. He didn't. My account of Santa's unavailability satisfied him.

On the bus to Nat and Ezra's. The bus passes a stop. Isaac gets excited.

Isaac: This is the 277. It should stop at that stop. Maybe it was closed. [Thinks a bit]. Maybe no one wanted to get on.

On the bus he spells out the 'edistration' letters on cars. [Registration]. Later:

Isaac: Can I count to a hundred?
Me: I think so.
Isaac: Can I count to a thousand?
Me: Mm. Bit tricky.
Isaac: How many numbers in a thousand?
Me: A thousand. That's what a thousand is. A thousand numbers.

He asks to go on my shoulders but uses a code based on the initial sound of shoulders. 'Shuh, shuh, shuh.' Outside Nat and Ezra's house: 'Can I go on your shuh, shuh, shuh?' If I refuse he complains of fatigue or a bad leg.

'I want go on your shuh, shuh, shuh.' And up he goes ...

Playing Pictionary, he saw a new word 'soup.' He spelled out the letters and said 'sowp' rhyming 'owp' with the *owp* in 'cowpat.' 'Sowp.' He didn't recognize it as 'soup.'

Christmas Eve 2011 (Aged 5 yrs, 6 months) I went to buy a present for Celia 'from Isaac.' A tea-caddy. I showed it to Isaac and Leo and swore them to secrecy. 'It's a special box for tea. Don't tell Celia what it is.' Upstairs I wrapped the tea-caddy with Isaac's help. Celia came home, desperate to know what her present was – immediately. She couldn't wait. She heard him coming downstairs. 'Did you leave holes in the paper so I can see what it is?' she called out. He brought the wrapped present into the sitting-room. I overheard this:

Celia: That looks a bit strange.
Isaac: [picking up his mum's suspicions] It looks horrible. [But remembering loyalty to his dad] No, you will love it.
Celia: A biscuit tin?
Leo: It's for putting ...
Isaac: Sshshshsh!!!

Dec 24th 2011 Leo had chicken pox so we didn't see him for two days. Then: –

Me: Is Leo coming today?
Isaac: Yes. His chicken pox is finished.

Leo arrives.

Isaac: Let's go upstairs.
Leo: What for?
Isaac: Play bums.

Dec 27th Leo announces: 'Do you know how old God is? He's two thousand.' I told Isaac I didn't believe in God. He seemed scandalised so I told him I believed in the universe. 'I believe in everything.'

Isaac: Then you believe in God.

Dec 28th 2011 Restaurant. Isaac eating Smarties, drinking apple juice, awaiting the arrival of a pizza, shortly before being taken by Thames Clipper to a railway station for an overnight trip to Kent with his mother and his best friend at Christmas.

Isaac: 'I wish I didn't have a bad life.'

Jan 4th 2012 Isaac is left alone at home for the first time ever while Celia goes shopping. (I was out.) I asked him about this later. He said he was worried someone might steal him.

Me: No one's going to steal you. Even though you're worth a lot of money.
Isaac: Do I cost a lot of money?
Me: Yes, but you're worth it. You're the gift that keeps on receiving.
Isaac: How much do I cost?
Me: Blimey. Er, loads.
Isaac: Infinity pounds.

Jan 5th Isaac, me and Celia reading his book of kings & queens. He reaches Henry VIII.

Isaac: Can you have this much wives?
Me: Yes. You can have a new wife if your wife dies or there's another way, if you get fed up and say, that's it, go away and find someone else. That's called divorce.
Isaac: Why don't you say that, Mummy?
Celia: Because I love Daddy really, except when he's being really annoying.

Isaac: Is jee jee eff eff a swearing word.

Me: GGFF?
Isaac: Is it a swearing word?
Me: Say it.
Isaac: Jee jee eff eff.
Me: No.
Isaac: It sounds like a swearing word.

['Good game finished fast' – internet jargon]

Also on **Jan 5**th

Isaac: What can't you burn?
Me: People.
Isaac: What happens if you burn metal?
Me: It just gets hotter. Or melts.
Isaac: Glass?
Me: Same. Not everything burns.
Isaac: What doesn't burn?
Me: Water. ...

[He recognises this information from somewhere]

Isaac: Ah.
Me: And when the fire brigade come, they put water on the fire and it goes out.
Isaac: What if you just put on a teeny drop?
Me: Not enough. See the fire in the fire-place? If it burnt out of control we'd fill that bucket [the coal scuttle] and throw it on the fire and it would go out.
Isaac: What if we threw it [the coal scuttle full of water] on the sun?
Me: Wouldn't be enough. And if it was enough, and the sun went out, we'd all die.

Jan 7th **2012** Isaac, the post-Christmas philosopher.

Isaac: Is Fr Christmas dead?

Me: No, he's got to get all the presents for next Christmas.
Isaac: Is he the same as God?
Me: No.
Isaac: But God doesn't die. And no one has seen God. And no one has seen Fr Christmas.

[Good point!]

In my study. I hear a fighting game next door with Nat, Ezra, Isaac and Leo. Separate bouts being arranged by Isaac with a whistle to start the fight. Isaac selects Leo as his first opponent.

Leo: Stop pushing me, Isaac. You're trying to make me lose.
Isaac [evidently redoubling his exertions]: That's the whole point. That is the whole point of fighting. I'm trying to make you lose.

Jan 8th Nat and Ezra's mum, Joy, has tickets to watch gymnastics at the O2. Isaac is excited.

Me: You know what gymnastics means? Exercise with no clothes on.
Isaac: No pants?
Me: Nothing. That's how they did it in the old days. Gymnastics is like a circus and a game as well. Your team has to get more points than the other team. Do you want to see that?
Isaac: I'll be too embarrassed.

[He thought spectators were naked too]

Jan 22nd Isaac watching Michael Jackson's O2 rehearsal video. *Beat It* starts and Michael is dancing. 'I don't like that. He's touching his willy!'

Jan 23rd (Age 5 yrs, 7 months) Isaac on the bus home wants to know which jobs are done 24 hours a day.

Isaac: Do doctors go to sleep?

Me: Yes, night doctors do the job when they're tired.
Isaac: Fire brigade?
Me: Yes, they have special firemen at night.
Isaac: Police?
Me: Yes.
Isaac: All the 999 people.
Me: That's it.
Isaac: Builders?

A woman sitting nearby laughed, good-naturedly, but Isaac didn't like being laughed at and he didn't pursue the line of enquiry. Next he asked about the police coming at night to catch a baddie at a shop 'that's been robbed.' I said that the police would arrive if the shopkeeper called them. Then he asked, what if the shop *hadn't* been robbed. I said that was bad and the shopkeeper would go to prison.

Isaac: But the police don't know. They haven't been to the shop before.

I asked him if he had a hard life:
'Yes.'
'Why?'
'I work all the time.'

He's always asking about bosses. Who has a boss? Why does everyone need a boss?

Jan 28th 2012 Isaac on theology. We're talking about the Nativity. 'How come baby Jesus came out of the mummy's tummy when there wasn't a hospital?'

[doing a little dance of celebration as he asks it]

Me: Good question. Some people say there were dinosaurs with the shepherds and the Wise Men because they believe that dinosaurs were alive when Jesus was alive.

I thought he might find this funny, or weird, but he says:

Isaac: Might have been.

Jan 29th Isaac bouncing on the sofa. 'What's it called that smoke, in the theatre, that smoke. What's it called?'
Me: Dry ice.
Isaac: How do you make that smoke?
Me: Special machine.
Isaac: Can I get one?
Me: No. Too expensive.
Isaac: Ohhhh.
Me: When you're older you can buy yourself one. When you're an adult.
Isaac: And I've got all your money. Yayyy!

He leaps jubilantly off the sofa.

Feb 4th Isaac on military build-ups.

Isaac: Do you know a lot about the war?
Me: Yes.
Isaac: You never know when there's gonna be another war.
Me: True. Who told you that?
Isaac: No. You do know – because the alarm goes blooahh bloooah bloooah.

Feb 10th 2011 He says, 'Rudi and Django's dad is very fixable. And very choppable.'

Meaning my brother is good at fixing and chopping.

Random question Feb 17th 'How old you goan be when I'm 20?'

Answer – '63.'

Feb 18th Passing the Victoria pub. He reads the name. 'The Victoria. Is that in Victorian times?'

On the bus.

Isaac: How do you get famous?
Me: Do something no one else can do.

Dalston station. 'What if I stood on my toe-nails would that make me famous?'

Feb 19th 2012 Mad questions. 'Do the police have to pay for police cars?' 'Do burglars have bosses?' 'Do you like things real or pretending?'

Isaac: Can the police go to jail?
Me: Yes, if they do something bad.
Isaac: Smoking?

He thinks smoking is a crime. And eating sugar.

He's entering a 'woff-u' phase. Every question starts 'woff-u?'

Isaac: Woff-u do a made-up job?
Me: Then you don't really have a job. But you could start a business. You could make cakes and sell them along the street. That would be your job.
Isaac: And your boss would be your brain.

At the playground he was showing me a game based on his prowess and daring.

Isaac: Do you think I can slide down there?
Me: Yes.
Isaac: Nooooo!

He wanted me to deny that he could go down a particular slide.

Isaac: Do you think I can slide down there?
Me: No.
Isaac: Why?
Me: Hurt yourself.

He descended the slide without injury.

Feb 23rd 2012 (5 yrs, 8 months) Isaac approaches the kitchen where I'm sitting.

Isaac: I know you're not going to say yes.
Me: What?
Isaac: I know you're not going to say yes.
Me: To what?
Isaac: Can we saw something?
Me: Sorry, mate.

He wanted to saw something valuable in half.

A roaring fire in the grate. I'm tidying up and tossing random bits and bobs onto the blaze. On the sofa, Isaac finds two £20 notes belonging to Celia. I pick up the notes.

Isaac: Don't throw it on the fire!

He genuinely feared that I might burn £40.

Written in his exercise book. 'My mum noas diffrent cins of dogs.'

Feb 29th 2012

Isaac: Can a girl have a sister?
Me: Yes.
Isaac: Can a boy have a brother?
Me: Yes. I've got a brother. Who?

[long frowning pause]

Isaac: Trevelyan?

March 1st Isaac very tired. Celia says he can eat anything he wants.

Isaac [disbelieving]: Anything?
Celia: Anything!
Isaac: Ice cream.
Celia: No.
Isaac: See?

Oddly he was more pleased that Celia had confirmed her prejudice against ice cream than he was by the prospect of eating ice cream. He didn't press to be given ice cream.

March 3rd

Isaac: Woff my whole life was a dream?
Me: Some people think that it is. ... Hey, Celia,

[As she enters]

Me: Isaac's a solipsist. He just said, "what if my whole life was a dream?"
Celia: Ooh.
Isaac: And I was in your tummy still.

March 4th Leo on the bus. 'I don't love anyone but my mum.'

March 5th On the bus, playing rhymes. Lane, plane, main, pain. Isaac asks about blame which he thinks is a bad word and possibly even a 'swearing word.' He makes up a rhyme for 'plain' which sounds like Kobain.

Me: Kobain?
Isaac: Is that a word?
Me: It's a person. He died.

Isaac: How did he die?
Me: Took a gun and shot himself in the head.
Isaac: What did he look like?
Me: Not good, after that.
Isaac: But what did he look like?
Me: Er, blond hair.
Isaac: Did he look like me?
Me: No.

Isaac's hair is blond but I changed the subject. Isaac started repeating other words. He tentatively tried to say bullshit pronouncing it boshit. A stern look from me. He decided to halve the word and bowdlerized it to 'bosh.'

Isaac: Bosh. Is that a word?
Me: It's the French word for German. Posh is a word.
Isaac: Posh.
Me: You've heard 'posh.' You know what it means?
Isaac: Yes.
Me: What?
Isaac: Strict.
Me: No. It means you've got too much money.
Isaac: And handsome?
Me: No, it doesn't mean handsome. Posh people can be ugly.

He asked if a girl can have a girlfriend.
Me: Yes.
Isaac: A boy can have a boyfriend?
Me: Yes.
Isaac: A boy can marry a boy?
Me: Yes. But can a boy marry a sheep?

Amused and outraged.

Isaac: No! You can't marry animals. Or things.

He's interested in prison sentences and he understands that the punishment reflects the severity of the offence. He suggests that if you said 'a swearing word' the police would come but wouldn't arrest you. I tell him that you'd go to prison for a long time if you killed people.

Isaac: Forever?
Me: Yes, some people go to prison forever if they're very dangerous.

He asks about Jack the Ripper, whose name he forgets, but he calls him 'the man who killed lots of ladies.' When did he die? How old was he? And so on. I can't answer because Jack the Ripper wasn't caught. Isaac doesn't understand. Perhaps to console himself, he constructs an elaborate scenario in which a bad person got into Jack the Ripper's house while he was asleep.

'He put stuff on the knife he used to kill lots of ladies and next time he used the knife the stuff poisoned his hand and he died.'

He puts energy and commitment into this explanation. He hates the idea that Jack the Ripper evaded capture and that his identity is still unknown. Leaving the bus he asks, 'would you go to prison if you stole the whole world?' He knows this is an absurd question. 'Yes,' I say.

March 6th 2012 My birthday. Isaac leaves for school. 'How about we'll make a cake for your birthday and we won't put a candle. We'll just splat it on your face?'

March 10th Isaac wakes from a dream and says to Celia. 'If we went into a Pyramid it would be kind to leave the gold.'

('kind not to remove the gold.')

Isaac: What film do you know when you were little?
Me: *Chitty Chitty Bang Bang.*

Isaac: Did you have the DVD?
Me: No.
Isaac: Did you have *Star Wars* when you were little?
Me: No. It came out when I was 13.
Isaac: Did you see it when you were 18?
Me: I've never seen it.
Isaac: Did you read the book?
Me: I didn't know there was a book.
Isaac: There isn't. I don't know.

Unanswerable question #300. 'What's past heaven?' 'What's past the sky?' 'What's past space?'

March 26th 2012 (Aged 5 yrs, 9 months)

Isaac: Who discovered God?
Me: Lots of people. Have you heard of Matthew, Mark, Luke and John?
Isaac: Is she a singer?

Unanswerable question #301 'What can a bomb not bomb?'

March 30th We're going to see Grandpa in hospital.

Isaac: Same hospital as before?
Me: Yes.
Isaac: Same room?
Me: No. He's not very well. He may be asleep.
Isaac: Is he going to have a operation?
Me: No. No more operations.
Isaac [amused disbelief]: Why's he in hospital?

Next day.

Me: Do you want to see Grandpa again?
Isaac: Yes.

Which surprised me. Then he tells me he found him a bit scary-looking and he refers to him in the present tense. So we talk about him as if he were with us.

Isaac: Why's his mouth open?
Me: He's sleeping. He's in a very deep sleep.
Isaac: I don't think he looks like Grandpa in that hospital.
Me: I don't think he's going to get better.
Isaac: He might do.

This prompts memories of Davy Jones, of The Monkees, who recently died – as did Whitney Houston. 'Why does every singer die by heart attack?'

My father died and I consoled Isaac, half-jokingly. 'You've had a tough year, Isaac. First one Grandpa dies. And then another.'

[He turns to me, all eagerness]

Isaac: Grandma?

April 4th 2012

Isaac: What's your boss called?
Me: Liz.
Isaac: Why's he called Lid?

April 5th On a walk. Isaac reads a sign. 'Nottick. Nottick. What's nottick?' [Notice]

Later, Isaac gives Leo a tiny easter egg.

Isaac: Do you like that?
Leo: Yeah. Tastes of cocoa.
Isaac: Ezra doesn't like chocolate.
Leo: Oh come on.
Isaac: He's learning to get used to it.

Leo: My supply teacher doesn't like chocolate.
Isaac: I'm goan kill her. No. I'm goan shove it down her mouth.

He's obsessed with the police and keeps asking 'will the police come?' in reference to any misdemeanour. He pronounces 'charged' and 'touched' with two syllables. Charge *ed* and touch *ed*.

April 11th Me, Isaac and Leo.

Isaac: Can you have brain cancer?
Me: Yes.
Isaac: Bottom cancer?
Me: Yes.
Isaac: Booby cancer?
Me: Breast cancer, yes.
Isaac: Willy cancer?
Me: Yes, anything that's alive.
Leo: Plant cancer?
Me: No, OK, anything that's alive on a human being.

April 12th 2012

Isaac: What do you pay for a hospital?
Me: Nothing.
Isaac: Do they pay you?
Me: No.
Isaac: What!??

April 13th En route to Aberystwyth.

Isaac: Why are there lots of mountains in Wales?
Me: Don't know, maybe they're old volcanoes.
Isaac: What can a volcano not burn?
Me: It can burn anything. Metal, paper. Anything.
Isaac: The sun?
Me: No.

Isaac: [triumphant] See!

April 15th Aberystwyth at breakfast. Isaac quizzes me about the moral values of numbers.

Isaac: Is odd bad?
Me: No.
Isaac: Is even good?
Me: No. They're not good or bad, they're just numbers.
Isaac: Odd is bad because you can't share odd.

A new ambition – fame. 'If I went to the moon would I be famous?'

Isaac the great literalist:

Me: When we go to Devon you can have a ride in Trevelyan's tractor.
Isaac: Can I drive it?
Me: Maybe he'll let you.
Isaac: But I'm not allowed.
Me: Not on the road. But you can if it's your own land.
Isaac: But it's not my land.

April 20th Celia and I getting him dressed, prior to going out. 'Put my socks on,' he says.

We put his socks on. He lies back.

Isaac: I'm like a king. And you are my servants.

April 28th 2012 (Aged 5 yrs, 10 months) Leo has memorised many of the world's capitals. He enjoys being quizzed about this and Isaac gets jealous. He tells me out loud to ask Leo countries whose capitals are obscure.

Isaac: What one doesn't he know?
Me: No, Isaac. We're trying to learn them not catch him out.

I ask Leo a few capitals in Europe and Asia. Leo gets them all right. Then south America.

Me: Capital of Venezuela?
Leo: I don't know.
Isaac [whispers to me]: Don't tell him!
Me: Caracas. What's the capital of Bolivia?
Leo: I don't know.
Isaac: Don't tell him!
Me: La Paz.
Leo: Oh La Paz, yes.

Later ... Leo, Isaac and me.

Me: Which is better, Catholic or church of England?
Leo: I don't know. You're a Catholic, Lloyd.
Me: Well, yes. Once a Catholic and all that.

Isaac perks up & makes a momentous theological announcement.

Isaac: I want to be a Catholic.
Me: OK. I can take care of that. I'll baptise you right now. But it's not easy being a Catholic. You have to go to church for a whole hour every Sunday. Forever.
Isaac: And if you don't?
Me: You go to hell.

Truth dawns.

Isaac: You don't go to church every week, Daddy.
Me: Right. So I might go to hell. Actually I think God is good. He wouldn't make hell.

Isaac still disturbed by what he's heard.

Isaac: I don't want you to go to hell, Daddy.

He says this twice. Arms himself with an imaginary gun.

Isaac: I will shoot God. Peow! Peow!

After a short lull, Isaac has a private word with Leo.

Isaac: OK, I'll tell you something. What if the world is actually God's bottom?
Leo: I can't smell the poo.
Isaac: And you know what rain is? His wee!

May 1st 2012 I collected Isaac for the first time since the end of last term, i.e. three days before Grandpa died. 'Remember when I came last time? The last day of school. And the next day we went to see him in hospital. And then two days later he died.'
Isaac: Did he miss the Olympic games?
Me: Well, yeah. He's dead.
Isaac: When he was a child.

[referring to the 1948 London Olympics]

May 4th Out of nowhere, Isaac suddenly says 'is Father Christmas real?' I say he is real. But clearly it's only a matter of time.

Isaac on the computer doing educational research: 'what are sinks made of? What are knives made of?'

Isaac: What's above the clouds?
Me: The sky.
Isaac: What's above the sky?
Me: Outer space.
Isaac: Out of space?

May 13th 2012 'Daddy. In the olden days was one penny very expensive?' [valuable]

Me: Yes.

Isaac: Enough to buy a cat?
Me: Enough to buy a house.
Isaac: What does zero pence look like?
Me: Nothing.

Isaac sets a quiz for me and Celia. 'This question is for both of you.' Three questions. 'Why did God make the world? Why are there different religions? Why are there different countries?'

May 15th Pillow-fighting. He has a bath on condition that more pillow-fighting will follow. After the bath he's very tired so I re-negotiate the pillow-fighting deal. He goes nuts. 'You can't break the deal. I hate you, Daddy. I'm going to hate you till you die and I'm not even going to come to your funeral.'

More like this. He reminds me that I promised pillow-fighting. So I agree to two minutes more. He relents, up to a point, but still nurses his anger.

Isaac: I still hate you and I'm not going to come to your funeral.
Me: Oh dear.
Isaac: Is Grandma going to come?

May 29th (Aged 5 yrs, 11 months) Isaac's teacher, Miss Gimlett, is a Kiwi and I keep asking Isaac to ask her who first climbed Mt Everest. He keeps forgetting. 'I'll ask her tomorrow. And if I don't, I'll kill myself.'

He was given a book about blindness which prompts a new ambition. 'I want to learn the dot alphabet!'

He's intrigued by Nat's pronunciation. 'He doesn't say moustache, he says moo stash.'

He contemplates our trip to Devon. He's convinced that it's just seven stops on the train.

Me: It's about 200 miles.
Isaac: Is it all the way from heaven to New Zealand?

June 10th 2012 Isaac wants to read my record of his sayings. After reviewing the last entry, he asks me again how far it is to heaven.

Me: There's no such place.
Isaac: There is! That's where dead people go to.

We discuss how far it is to heaven and whether it's closer than New Zealand. 'Is it that far or is it less than that?'

After a walk, about to have meringues: 'has everyone had a meringue in the whole world?'

On the way to *The Lion, the Witch and the Wardrobe*, Isaac gets a tube map and tries reading all the station names with the map upside down. He demonstrates this to me. I'm not sure if he's cheating. He asks me about the size of continents and he's surprised that America isn't the largest. He's building up to tell me about Magic World – a fantasy invented by him and Leo. He says Magic World is bigger than all the continents, even Asia. I should have shown more interest in Magic World or at least asked him where it is. Undeterred, he says: 'I'll tell you where Magic World is. Magic World is on the other side of the world ... [pause] ...where is the other side of the world?'

I told him I was going to quote his thoughts about *The Lion, the Witch and the Wardrobe* in the magazine. This shut him up. All he said, throughout the show, was 'I don't like that Aslan.' At the end he said, 'it wasn't that long.' Early on there was a scary bit where the Queen whipped her horses with lots of noise. Some kids were frightened. I turned to him.

Me: Was that scary?
Isaac: No. Was it scary for you?

He reads an advert on a crowded tube.

Isaac: What's that mean? Luh, oh, suh, suh.
Me: LOSS. It means hair loss.
Isaac: Mummy's got hair loss.
Me: Er, well only two tiny bits. She's not bald.
Isaac: No. That man's not bald –

He's pointing at the photo of the slightly bald chap in the picture.

Me: No. But he's worried.

June 20th 2012 Isaac still obsessed with becoming famous.

Isaac: Whoff you were famous and you didn't know!?

[Pause]

Isaac: They would tell you.

June 21st Bus ride. He talks about our descent from apes but doesn't say it in explicit terms, he mimes it. 'Because we used to be …' [scratching armpits and going 'ooh-ooh, ah-ah.'] I pour scorn on this theory as I'm sceptical about evolution.

Me: You don't believe *that* do you? We used to be monkeys?
Isaac: They wrote about it in books.
Me: Yeah, but they don't know, do they?

He picks up fast on my scepticism and criticises evolutionist writers.

Isaac: Were they once a monkey and they remembered? I don't think so!

Discussing where Barack Obama lives, I say 'the White House' which he thinks refers to a slapstick show, *Wipe Out*.

Age **Six**

July 3rd 2012 (Aged 6 years, 0 months) Passing a ticker in Canary Wharf showing stock prices. He asks what they're for. 'The value of money in banks.' He wants more info and I notice that they're US prices.

Me: Those are American banks. The banks are still open in America.
Isaac: What time is it in America?
Me: 12 o'clock. Lunchtime.
Isaac: Do they have to have lunch at the same time in America?

I laugh. He looks hurt, not pleased. He asks about nuclear weapons. Celia had told him there were special shelters during bomb strikes. He asks how you know when a nuclear war is imminent.

Me: They have to press a button. A special red button.
Isaac: Is it on the wall?
Me: No – in a suitcase.
Isaac: A clothes suitcase?

He keeps asking me to pronounce words like 'ice' in an American accent.

On nuclear weapons, I told him they were made from a dangerous metal.

Me: They could blow up the whole of London.
Isaac: Is that the whole country?

I told him that only a few countries had them. He offered to name them and his first guess was New Zealand, where Miss Gimlett's from. Then he guessed Australia, America and Africa. I gave him the list. He'd heard of them all except Israel and Pakistan but he repeated them correctly. On the bus he read random traffic signs.

Isaac: What's zon? Zon. What's zon? Slow zon.
Me: Zone. It means area.

'Zon' reminded him of 'scones' which he made last week.

When in a rage he shouts at me. 'Just get out of this house!'

July 12th 2012 Googling Michael Jackson he finds pictures of Neverland. He's seen properties advertised on-line.

Isaac: Is it for sale?
Me: No.
Isaac: Can we buy it?
Me: No.
Isaac: Why not?
Me: Can't afford it.

He sees the Neverland funfair which he knows about.

Isaac: Did he really build it for kids?
Me: Yeah.
Isaac: How much did Michael Jackson love kids?
Me: Good question. Ask Mummy.

July 18th – with his new computer looking at an advert.

Isaac: What's nuh, eye, luh, eh?
Me: Nile. It's a river.
Isaac: What's deeth?
Me: Death. Death on the Nile.

July 21st Strange questions about the most famous this or that.

'What's the famousest singer in the world?'
'What's the famousest country in the world?'

'Which continent is best at sport?'

Watching cricket, England v S Africa, he wanted to know who I supported. 'Which side are you?' And he kept saying 'I really want England to win.' I tried to explain the rules. He wondered who got most points. I said 'runs' not points. He was intrigued that a boundary was 'four.'

Isaac: How many if you hit it in the audience?
Me: Six.
Isaac: How many if you hit it out of the place?
Me: Same. Six. Six is the most.

This disappointed him. He repeatedly asked if you get scores of eight, ten, five or three. He liked the idea that a catch was good. But he thought every appeal meant that a catch had been taken. Explaining the TV replay system was even harder. I told him that the game lasted five days. 'Including overnight?' he asked.

I said that Americans don't play cricket and they think English people are mad for devising a game that lasts five days. This fascinated him. He wanted to know if I supported the American view that the English are mad.

July 23rd (Aged 6 yrs, 1 month) Jamie, from across the road, arrives. Leo is already here. Leo quizzes Jamie.

Leo: How old are you?
Jamie: Six.
Leo: When were you six?
Jamie: At my birthday, at my birthday. I get older once it's my birthday.

Leo expected him to name a month.

Devon. The Royal Oak in Dunsford. Jeremy Clarke quizzed Leo, 6, on capital cities. He tried all the tough ones, Australia, America, Thailand, Ulan Bator. Leo got them all right. Jeremy asked, 'Tibet?'

Leo: That's not really a country.

Leo wrote a list of things that Isaac would take on his plane to Morocco. And a list of things he couldn't take including drugs. Isaac doesn't know what a drug is but he's seen TV documentaries about customs officers confiscating drugs at airports. In the garden he called me over, away from the others. He looked eager and anxious, and slightly embarrassed, as he asked me a question in an urgent whisper. 'Is raggy and dummy a drug?' I said no. He told me not to tell anyone he'd asked that.

Aug 5th Strange question. 'When one person is older and one person is younger, can they catch up?'

Looking at a Michael Jackson website. 'Was he born in one nine five eight? [1958]

Aug 6th 2012 Preparing to go to a fair where spectators could try out Olympic sports. He's with Oriel, 18. 'I'm going to do shooting.'
Oriel: Who are you going to shoot? Are you going to shoot me?
Isaac: No.
Oriel: Who are you going to shoot?
Isaac: The audience.

Aug 8th Celia upstairs with Isaac, three hours before their flight to Africa.

Celia: Let's get you dressed. And then we're almost ready to go.
Isaac: To?
Celia: Morocco.
Isaac: For?
Celia: A holiday.

Isaac: How many days?
Celia: Seven.
Isaac: Seven plus seven is?
Celia: 14.

Isaac was unaware that the holiday was imminent. Nor was he greatly excited by his first trip to Africa. After he came back, I told him that London had held the Olympics three times – more than any other city. He was pleased. 'So England is the goodest sporter in the world.'

He showed me a picture of himself, taken by Celia, in a shop, trying on a red Michael Jackson jacket. 'It had a very lot of zips.'

Aug 24th (Aged 6 yrs, 2 months) Coming back from Leo's he asked me if spies are real. I said yes. He asked how you know if someone's a spy. I told him you couldn't tell. Anyone could be a spy. If a spy was asked if they were a spy they might say no and not mean it.

Me: Ask me if I'm a spy.
Isaac: Are you a spy?
Me: No. ... Now, do you know if I'm a spy or not?

He didn't reply but he understood the complication I was illustrating.

Aug 27th 2012 Ginger beer. Isaac, prompted by jealousy of Leo who claims to like ginger beer, persuades Celia to buy him ginger beer. He comes home and I open the bottle. 'You might not like it. It's spicy,' I said. Isaac drinks.

Isaac: Mmmm! Nice! [Beat] OK. It is not nice but I am going to drink it.

Random question. 'How old are you going to be when you die?'

Isaac: How old is the oldest person in the world?
Me: 110 maybe.
Isaac: If I lived to 120 would I be famous?

Questions on the tube. 'Who's the poorest man in the world?'

Isaac: Who is the richest man in the world?
Me: It changes all the time.
Isaac: I mean today.
Me: The man who makes the computers.
Isaac: Does he still live?
Me: Yes.
Isaac: How old?
Me: About sixty.
Isaac: Does he still make computers?
Me: Other people do it for him.
Isaac: Why did your dad marry two people?
Me: He got fed up with one.
Isaac: How old were you when your dad married Nuala?

Walking back from the tube.

Isaac: How long does it take to build a house?
Me: A small house like that, about three months.
Isaac: How long does it take to build half a house?
Me: Six weeks.
Isaac: How long does it take to build a quarter of a house?

Sept 6th Filling in a form about donating blood. First he thought the hospital would give me blood. Other way round, I said. He asked me how much I'd give. I pointed to my large coffee cup. 'That much, or a bit more.' He asked how long it would take. 'Half an hour.' He didn't want me to complete the form.

Isaac: Don't do it. Don't do it.
Me: Why?

Isaac: Just don't do it.
Me: OK.

[Isaac not satisfied]

Isaac: Deal?
Me: OK.

[We shake]

Isaac: Because that would be a waste of blood.

Sept 7th 2012 A morning quiz, with me trying to work.

Isaac: What's the coldest place in the world?
Me: South pole, Isaac. You know that.
Isaac: Does it snow a lot?
Me: Yes.
Isaac: Every day?
Me: Yes.
Isaac: All night?
Me: Sometimes.
Isaac: How long are the nights?
Me: Six months.
Isaac: Mmm.
Me: Long time, isn't it.
Isaac: But does it seem quick?

Sept 9th Walking to Leo's.

Isaac: Who's the oldest person in the world?
Me: Don't know.
Isaac: They have to be still alive.
Me: Well, yes.
Isaac: Or they won't be famous.

Sept 10th 2012 Isaac on the tube to his new school, Hill House International, in Chelsea. I'm reading about the pre-Socratics. 'The first scientists,' I say.

Isaac: Did people used to think the world was flat?
Me: Yes.
Isaac: But it's round.
Me: Yes.
Isaac: Who was the first man in space?
Me: Yuri Gagarin.
Isaac: Was he the first man to know the world was round?
Me: No, the Egyptians knew it.
Isaac: Greeks?
Me: Yes.
Isaac: Romans?
Me: Yes.
Isaac: Knights?
Me: Yes. Well, maybe some didn't.

This is Isaac's division of epochs: Egyptians, Greeks, Romans, knights.

Sept 14th He has his great-grandpa's field binoculars. 'Are these war glasses?'

Going to Leo's I gave him a conker. He was desperate to find a conker tree. 'Is that a conker tree, is this a conker tree, is that a conker tree?' I found one and pointed out its smooth leaves shaped like a tear. But it had no conkers. Then he claimed to see conker trees everywhere.

Isaac: That's a conker tree
Me: No.
Isaac: That's a conker tree.
Me: No, it's got pointy leaves.

Isaac: That's a conker tree.
Me: No, it's got pointy leaves.
Isaac: That's a conker tree.
Me: No.

Clutching his conker.

Isaac: Whoff the whole world was made of conkers?
Me: Er, well, Isaac ...
Isaac: Whoff the whole world was made of everything? It is! Made of grass, made of scooters, made of trees ...

Sept 22nd 2012 Saturday morning. Isaac tells Leo that Celia is going to take them on the Thames Clipper to the Cabinet War Rooms.

Isaac: Do you know Dr Who?
Leo: Yeah.
Isaac: We're going to a museum where they planned the first wide war. No we're going to a museum where they planned the second world war.
Leo: Where is it?
Isaac: I think it's in Westminster. And we're going on the boat.
Leo: Oooh.

[Pause]

Leo: Do you know the Shard, yeah? It hasn't been built yet but it is going to be built.
Isaac: Daddy, has the Shard been built?
Me: Yes.
Leo: My friend told me it hasn't been built.

[Pause]
Leo: My dad told me I have been to Ibiza.
Isaac: Where's or-beeth-uh?

Leo: In Spain. It's one of the tiniest islands.
Isaac: Have you been to Spain?
Leo: Yeah.
Isaac: What's it like?
Leo: When I was little I had a little dog and it had Pedro on it.
Isaac: There's someone in my school called Pedro.
Leo: Is he from Spain?
Isaac: Yeah.

[Ending the discussion about Spain]

As they leave for the War Rooms, Isaac is standing on the pavement and I'm on the doorstep. I ask him who won the war. He gives a wry and very satisfied grin and digs his thumb twice towards his chest.

Sept 23rd 2012 (Aged 6 years, 3 months)

Isaac: What's the furthest-est country?
Me: New Zealand.
Isaac: I thought it was Antarctica
Me: OK, but it's not really a country.

[Isaac has a brainwave and points a victorious finger at me]

Isaac: Space!
Me: OK, but that's not really a country either.
Isaac: We're nearer to space because we're at the top.

[He considers Santa]

Isaac: How long does Santa take to visit all the children?
Me: One night.
Isaac: Does he really come down the chimney or do your mum and dad give it to you?
Me: Santa.

[He's satisfied with this. Or he feels it politic to suppress his doubts. Later, in the kitchen with Isaac pootling around, I tell Celia about his emerging Santa-scepticism]

Me: He just said, does Santa come down the chimney or do your mum and dad give you your presents?
Isaac: I just said it by mistake.

[He no longer believes. But he's pretending to – to please us]

Sept 27th Home on the tube. He talks about runaway trains. Or rather 'the' runaway train.

'How do you get on the runaway train?' and 'how do you get off the runaway train?'

He thinks it's specifically built as 'the runaway train' and this confusion crystallises in the question of embarkation. He asks about getting on and off the runaway train and how long it would keep going. 'Is it a steam train?' I explained that any train could become 'a runaway' if the brakes failed or the driver was ill. This didn't help. 'But how do you get off the runaway train?' And, referring to the tube train we're on, 'is this a runaway train?'

Sept 29th Talking about blood. 'If you chopped your hand off would you die?'

Isaac: If you cut your hand how much blood would come out?
Me: All of it.

And

Isaac: What is old blood like?
Me: Brown.

'If you got all your blood and put it in a bowl for a day would it be brown?'

Strange questions: 'What's the famousest film in the world?'

'What's the mediumest building in the world?'
'What's the famousest language in the world?'
'Who's the youngest person in the world?'
'If I counted up to a million would I be famous?'

Sept 30th 2012 Isaac's aimless, tired talk on a Friday afternoon.

Isaac: How tall am I, am I more than 100 metres?
Me: Less. Less than two metres.
Isaac: Am I a foot?
Me: More. More like three and a half feet.
Isaac: Can I see how big I am related to you?

He comes over. I stand. He reaches to just above my waist.

Isaac: I am a bit as big as you.

He sits.

Isaac: How many years till I am as old as you?
Me: 43.
Isaac: Whoff I was 40?
Me: Three years. [I meant to say 9 years]

Oct 1st 2012 Isaac and Bertie solve the mystery of procreation.

Isaac: This is how Bertie Banks says the baby gets into the tummy. When you kiss, yeah, the seed goes into the mouth and then down the tube and into the tummy button.

He tells me this without asking for corroboration. Having said his piece he changes the topic.

Oct 2nd Isaac at home with a temperature. He asks about the war and my father's minor role. En route to his interview at the London

School of Economics, February 1945, he narrowly missed being hit by a V2 that landed on Holborn. Many dead.

Isaac: What would happen if the Germans won that war? Would we speak German?
Me: No, English.
Isaac: Mummy said we'd speak German.
Me: That's because she'd have joined the Germans. Not like me. I'd have joined the resistance. Mind you I wasn't around in the war.
Isaac: Your dad was. They nearly bombed him. Who tried to bomb him?
Me: Hitler.
Isaac: What hitler?
Me: There's only one Hitler.
Isaac: Did the hitler aim at your dad?
Me: Sort of.
Isaac: What kind of bomb was it?
Me: Rocket.
Isaac: A rocket bomb. That must have been a big, big bomb. Was your mum in the war?
Me: No.
Isaac: Not fighting, I mean. Did your dad fight?
Me: No.
Isaac: Was he a child?
Me: Yes.
Isaac: Why did they try to kill him?
Me: When the war started he was a child, and when it finished he was 16.
Isaac: How long was that war?
Me: Six years.
Isaac: Oh my gosh. Overnight?
Me: Did it carry on overnight.
Isaac: Yes ...

Me: Yes, it did.
Isaac: That means they must have been very tired. Did the hitler die?
Me: Yes.
Isaac: Do you know how he died?

I mime firing a gun at myself.

Isaac: Did he shoot himself?
Me: Yup.
Isaac: Why did he shoot his self?
Me: Cos he'd lost the war.
Isaac: Did he shoot himself in the head or ear?
Me: Mouth.
Isaac: Ooh. You know when I saw a film of the one who ... no but, but um, he thought. I saw a film and he ...someone shot himself in the mouth with a big, long gun.
Me: Oh.
Isaac: Has my school finished?
Me: Today, yes.
Isaac: How many wars did we win?
Me: Only the ones we talk about.
Isaac: I don't know every war though.

Isaac on London's history. 'I know what London Bridge used to look like. It had loads of houses and shops. But it couldn't open. And when it frozed people used to dance.'

When angry he now says 'I want you to just leave this house' or 'I can't wait till you leave this house.'

Oct 5th 2012 Isaac dislikes his new school. 'We only play one time. At Faraday we played two times.' His new favourite game is 'Scravel.' Leaving for school he needed something for Show & Tell and he chose 'the binoculuses.'

Back home, I poured him a supermarket apple juice. 'This is the apple juice at you get in pubs. I love this apple juice.' ['at' for 'that']

I play him the *Ride of the Walkyries* for the first time & his face lights up in angelic wonderment. 'This is in Dumbo!'

Oct 13th Isaac spots hypocrisy. Early evening. Celia flounces out in a strop. To torment Isaac she tells him she'll be gone all night. When he starts crying, she says she'll be back in ten minutes. She leaves. I console Isaac and tell him that Mummy won't be gone all night.

Me: She said she'll be back in 10 minutes.
Isaac: But she said it with a "no" look.

Interesting phrase for a deceitful expression. Isaac cheered up and Celia was back after 10 minutes.

October 20th 2012 Isaac asks about football.

Isaac: What football team do you like?
Me: Chelsea.
Isaac: What's the best football team?
Me: Chelsea are the best in Europe.
Isaac: I like that. And Scotland. I mean Ireland. And America. And the best team in the world. And your one.

Later, I'm working during a barrage of questions.

Isaac: How long would it take to get in the Space Shuttle to New Zealand?
Me: Not long.
Isaac: Ten minutes?
Me: About that.
Isaac: Devon?
Me: Oh, I don't know, Isaac.

Isaac: One second.
Me: Yes.
Isaac: Wow!

Nov 8th (Aged, 6 yrs, 4 months) Tube home. Isaac sees a photo that looks like Venice. Long conversations ensue about whether cars can drive in Venice and what they make in Venice. Is it TVs or computers, etc? Isaac assumes that manufacture and possession are identical and if Venetians don't make TVs they can't own them.

Isaac: Where do they make people?
Me: Well, they don't.
Isaac: Where was the first man made?
Me: They don't know.
Isaac: What was his name?
Me: In the Bible, he's called Adam.
Isaac: What about Jesus?
Me: He's later.
Isaac: Is Jesus God?
Me: Yes.
Isaac: Did they hammer him into that cross?
Me: Yes.
Isaac: Really into that cross?
Me: Yes.
Isaac: Was it real wood?
Me: Yes.
Isaac: Who hammered him into that cross?
Me: The Romans.
Isaac: I hate that. I would hammer them into that cross. I would get the needles and hammer them into that cross.
Me: Nails not needles.
Isaac: I said nails.
Me: You didn't.
Isaac: I did!

Isaac and Leo were playing at Susannah's with a boy of 9 called Hal. He resented the presence of two 6-year-olds so Isaac and Leo concluded he was 'bad' and discussed how to punish him. They typed, 'how to beat a bad boy' into Google. Later, Isaac: 'We squished his nuts.

We got off the tube at Stepney Green because of a suicide at Mile End. Which led to umpteen questions about ambulances and severed limbs as we walked home. None of which I was able to answer. We passed Queen Mary university – and at last – a new subject was born.

Isaac: What's that building?
Me: University.
Isaac: At university can you go to bed whenever you like?
Me: Yes.
Isaac: Stay up all night?
Me: Yes.
Isaac: What do they teach you?
Me: Anything and everything which is what university means.
Isaac: Magic?
Me: Probably.
Isaac: Yayyy!

A moment's hesitation, then

Isaac: Really?
Me: I expect so.

Isaac and Leo enact solemn pastiches of religious services. They build a temple on the floor from toys and pieces of wood which they identify as relics, e.g. 'the holy bird.' Isaac stands on a chair with a folder and chants a liturgy. During one recital they stumbled on a problem. Leo said that God was never alive. Isaac found this troubling and tried to dispute it.

Isaac: What about Jesus?
Leo: He wasn't God.
Isaac: Daddy, was Jesus God?
Me: Yes.
Leo: Your Dad's not an encyclopaedia
Isaac: But you know what he is. He's a journalist.

Reading about England's kings, all he wants to know is 'how did he die?' He has a strange reluctance to put 'by mistake' at the end of a sentence. He always sticks it in the middle, or near the start, but never right at the start. We reached Richard II. 'How did he die?' I told him, 'they got a spear and made it very hot in the fire and stuck it into him.'

'Did they by mistake do that?'

The detail of the fire probably made him think it was a mistake.

Nov 25th 2912 (Aged 6 yrs, 5 months) Isaac twirling on the roundabout, lying back. Night-time. 'I'm going back in time. Past the dinosaurs. Past when Jesus was alive. Past when he was on the cross. Past when he was born. Past colour. Past space.'
Me: Where are you?
Isaac: Nowhere!

Nov 26th Isaac enjoys 1960s music, especially *Yellow Submarine.*

Isaac: Who died of the Beatles?
Me: Two of them. John Lennon and George Harrison.
Isaac: Did the main singer die?
Me: Yes.
Isaac: How about the guitarer?
Me: George Harrison. Yes, he died too.

Nov 29th 'You know what? Bertie Banks did judo and he got down ten people.'

Watching Melinda's French video.

Isaac: Is she French or English?
Me: English.
Isaac: Why does she sound French?
Me: Pretending.
Isaac. She can pretend to be French well.

Dec 12th Thinking of Christmas in Devon with his cousins, Rudi and Django (seven years his senior.) Isaac: 'I prayed to God and said, "can Rudi and Django just play with me and not go anywhere else", cos they always do that.'

Dec 13th On the tube. 'If they cut your stomach open and you were still awake would you die?'

Dec 15th 2012 Isaac and Leo open a restaurant called 'Pianoch.' Isaac makes 'Turkish tea' from milk and chopped herbs (which he calls 'plants'). He offers me the tea. 'Taste it. It's nice. If that had hot water in it and no plants it would actually be Turkish tea.'

Dec 18th We build a toy car, solar-powered, given to Isaac by Nuala. The panel generates no energy. 'Maybe it's a hot day thing,' he says.

Train to Exeter to meet the cousins. Isaac's excitement increases. Ditto the daftness of his questions. To answer, I have to pull off feats of mental arithmetic which I officially find irksome but I enjoy in a strange way.

'When you're 99 how old will I be?'
'56.'
'When you're 100 how old will I be?'
'57.'
'When I'm 100 how old will you be?'
'143.'
'When you're a million how old will I be?'

'999,957.'

As we get nearer, the questions come thicker and faster.

Isaac: How much is a million miles?
Me: It's a million miles.
Isaac: But how much is it?
Me: You mean how long would it take to travel that far?
Isaac: Yes.
Me: Depends. Walking?
Isaac: Yes.
Me: Millions of years.
Isaac: In a rocket?
Me: Much quicker. A few days.
Isaac: From London to Devon?
Me: Doesn't make any difference what the route is. ....

At the Exeter hotel.

Isaac: People say the world's never going to end. I think it is going to end.
Me: Oh really?
Isaac: But we'll all be dead.
Me: Great. We're all going to die and the world's going to end. What cheery news, Isaac.

Dec 23rd 2012 (Aged 6 years, 6 months) Isaac was due to see *Life of Pi* with his cousins but it was cancelled because Celia, supported by Georgina, ruled that he was ill and a trip to the cinema might endanger his health further. He was fine. Celia didn't want to be stuck with G all evening. Isaac retired angrily to his bedroom where I tried to comfort him by pointing out that Celia and Georgina had confused the cinema with a leper colony or some other incubator of lethal germs. Celia came in and Isaac unleashed his full ire. 'This is the worst day of my life!'

En route to the farm we stopped for diesel.

Isaac: What's diesel?
Me: Like petrol.
Isaac: If you drank it would you die?
Me: It wouldn't do you any good, but you wouldn't die.
Isaac: A teeny bit?
Me: If you drank a teeny bit you'd be OK.

Dec 29th Long-house, Dartmoor. 'Who invented numbers?' he says. And corrects it. 'Who discovered numbers?'

Me: Well, we didn't really need to discover numbers. Because ....

I waved both hands, waggling the digits. He copied this.

Isaac: *Fingers* discovered them.

He pointed to the kitchen's massive stone walls.

Isaac: Are they bricks but made of stone?
Me: That's right.
Isaac: How did they carve them?
Me: With a chisel. You know what that is?
Isaac: Oh, I know. Like a thing for holding up tents.

Later, Isaac told Celia that in Dunsford he'd dreamed that both of us had died. Strange that he had this dream while staying at his most natural refuge (my brother's house) should death befall both his parents. I tried to reassure him that such dreams were normal.

'I dreamed that my mum had died,' I said. 'And then, even worse, in the dream, I thought that I'd killed her. Imagine that. Imagine dreaming that I'd killed my own mum and I thought it was all real.'

He looks at me.

Isaac: Do you want to kill your mum?

This, from a six-year-old, appears to dispose of a large chunk of Freud's psychological theory. I assumed that the core tenet – that dreams disclose unconscious desires – was unknown before Freud discovered it. Clearly Freud didn't make this discovery. It must be a commonplace observation that even small kids make. Either that or Isaac is a genius. The former explanation seems likelier.

Jan 1st 2013 Jeremy Clarke drives us to Widdecombe on the Moor. Isaac wants to know how time relates to distance. 'How long is four miles?'
Me: You mean how long does it take to go four miles?
Isaac: Yes.
Me: Depends how you're travelling.
Isaac: How about tiptoeing?
Me: Ten hours.
Isaac: Jogging?
Me: Twenty minutes.
Isaac: By space shuttle?
Me: A few seconds.
Isaac: Car?
Me: A car going at this speed, about 10 minutes.

At the pub, he's intrigued by the white ducks and ducklings splashing in the stream nearby. 'Have I ever touched a duck?' His mission 'to touch a duck' engrosses him intermittently during the afternoon and he sets off on stalking expeditions, creeping up on the ducklings to fulfil his great ambition. They always waddle away just in time. He says, 'I've never touched a duck' several times as if referring to some grave deprivation that demands correcting urgently.

Constant questions about wars, especially WW2. He keeps asking 'who else was on our team?' I told him Ireland didn't join because we'd fought a war with them. 'A secret war.' Centuries ago the English went to Ireland and announced that it belonged to England. He knew this already. 'Is that why the top of London is ours?'

He tried again with 'top of London' and it came out as 'top of England.' Eventually he said 'top of Ireland' – Northern Ireland.

Going to Exeter by cab, descending the long gorge between Morten and Dunsford he asks: 'Can you fall forever?'
Me: Not really.
Isaac: In space you can.

He finds a stone with a white band across the middle and he's convinced it contains a crystal. Can he look inside? What can cut stone? How do you break into stone? Might the crystal grow inside the stone if you leave it long enough?

Me: I don't know much about stones.
Isaac: Do you know someone who knows about stones?
Me: No.
Isaac: Twigger?

To Isaac, 'Twigger' means a man of almost superhuman intelligence and power (even though he couldn't drive out of a flood in West Bay to join us, as he'd promised, in our Dartmoor long-house.)

In the kitchen, musing on my mother's great age, of 87, he declares that no one is old until they're a hundred. Followed by the usual questions: 'When I'm 56 how old will you be?' and 'when I'm 149, how old will you be?' etc.

'What can cut stone?' he asks.
'Diamond?'

Jan 3rd 2013 Isaac looks at my laptop and sees an advert for holidays in Dubai. 'Dubai's for sale!'

Train journey. He draws a huge, complex map of Magic World and captions it 'Majic Wold.'

Constant fascination with the causes of death. He's telling Celia about Kitten, our new cat, not being able to survive if she doesn't have a garden. He fears Kitten will die without 'fresh air.' To me: 'Will you die if you don't get fresh air?'

Jan 4th 'Can you steal a pyramid?' Me: 'No.'

Isaac: How long does it take to build a pyramid?
Me: Hundreds of years.
Isaac: So by the time you've built it you're dead.

Jan 5th Science Museum. Me, Isaac and Leo looking at footage of V2 rockets being tested at Peenemunde. Isaac asked if that was the 'bomb that nearly landed on Grandpa.' Yes, I said. He immediately told an unconcerned Leo that his grandfather had survived a V2 rocket attack. To me: 'Did the English have them bombs?'

Me: No.
Isaac: That's just not really fair.

Jan 12th Saturday. Isaac watching a *Dr Who* episode set during the Roman Empire.

Isaac: How does the world explode?
Me: It doesn't.
Isaac: They say the sun will explode when the world ends.
Me: They think that it will, yes.
Isaac: When?
Me: Not for millions of years.
Isaac: Will we still be alive?
Me: What do you think?
Isaac: No.

Back he goes to *Dr Who.*

Sunday. He's due to go to Phil and Auntie Sarah's but he laments the lack of kids to play with. He can't understand Sarah's childlessness. 'She likes me so she should get a child.'

Back from Phil and Sarah's he tells me the bus journey was halted by 'a parade' which, he adds, was something to do with Turkey. (Militant Kurds marching through Dalston.) He calls a speaker system on a lorry 'a thing that louds it out.'

In the bath, out of nowhere. 'If you hit someone on the head with a shovel would they die?'

Tube. He reads a word in a newspaper. 'Towf. What's towf?' I tell him. Tough.

Other weird questions. As soon as he wakes up 'can a shark eat a shark?'

He dislikes my habit of asking him what he learned at school when I collect him.

16th Jan 2013 Celia brings him home.

Me: I'm not going to ask if you learned anything at school.
Isaac: You can if you like.
Me: What?
Isaac: Maths. And Ingerlish. [Slight difficulty over that word] We learned nouns.
Me: What's a noun?
Isaac: Something you can see and touch.
Me: OK. But it's not always something you can see and touch. What about unhappiness?
Isaac: If you write it you can see it.

[Touché!]

Jan 21st Tube home.

Isaac: What's eight divided by seven?
Me: Don't know. I'd need a calculator for that.
Isaac: Don't you know your divided bys?

He takes the newspaper and reads the weather symbols around the country. 'Sunny, cloudy, rainy, snowy. That's all the weathers. Oh and lightning.'

Outside, in the snow. 'I've got a special word for snow that hasn't been trodden on. Fresh snow.'

Me: And it's called virgin snow.
Isaac: That's a short word for 'not been trodden on'?

Me: When do you eat at school?
Isaac: Eleven o'clock.
Me: What do you have?
Isaac: Fruit. And something that's not healthy.

Meaning a chocolate bar. They give him bananas and blood oranges. He never eats bananas at home.

Me: Why don't you eat bananas at home?
Isaac: We're not allowed!

He thought I meant taking school bananas and eating them at home.

Big day. Isaac discovers Mary Seacole. The school took him to the National Army Museum where I'd taken him before. People taught him stuff. 'What about?'

Isaac: Florence Nightingale .... And Mrs, Mrs, ...
Me: Seacole?
Isaac: Yes.

Me: Who was better – Florence Nightingale or Mary Seacole?
Isaac: Florence Nightingale.
Me: Why?
Isaac: She helped people. And she was good at maths.

His new joy is to sit down with me and watch a DVD of his Wriggly Nativity play and provide a commentary. 'There's Bertie .... She's Japanese. ... I didn't like that boy but I like him now ... She's so shy!' etc.

Isaac waiting for Leo to arrive. Discovers he's due at 11am. He's satisfied. 'That's an hour and a half. That's as long as you have to type David Cameron.'

Meaning the time I take to write a political sketch.

Isaac the arch inquisitor. On the tube, I'm trying to read my book.

'Was there a Year One?' he asks.
'Yes.'
'Were people alive?'
'Yes.'
'What people?'
'I don't know what people, Isaac.'
'What *kind* of people. The Romans? The Saxons?'
'The Romans.'
'Was Jesus alive?'
'Yes.'
'Mary?'
'Yes.'
'You do know what people were alive!'
'Oh blimey.'

He asks me if 2013 will happen again. He hastily corrects this to 2012 which has just finished. I tell him I asked my parents that question in 1969! 'Will 1969 happen again?' I was six, as he is now. So in a sense it has come round again.

Tube. Lots of questions about charcoal which he pronounces 'charcle.' I suggested 'charcoal.' He said 'I like the word charcle.' He'd been drawing with it in school. It was warm today (**Jan 29th**) and I said 'it's like spring.' Isaac: 'It's quarter of spring.'

At Mile End, some older kids were mucking around. After we'd passed them, Isaac said, 'why do teenagers scream and throw things on the ground?'

He wanted to play *You Be The Judge* and started inventing dilemmas.

Isaac: How long would I go to prison for if I threw something at a police car and it crashed. One year?
Me: Less.
Isaac: One month?
Me: Maybe.
Isaac: A week?
Me: Maybe a week.
Isaac: A day?
Me: Maybe a bit more.
Isaac: But the police didn't die.
Me: A bit more than a day and less than a week.

Tube home. Isaac repeating info about planets that we've previously discussed.

Isaac: What's the first planet?
Me: Mercury.
Isaac: How long is a year on Mercury?
Me: 89 days?
Isaac: 86 days. I want to live there, you know why, because then it would be my birthday quicker. If I went there would I die?
Me: Yes. It's too hot.

Isaac: What if I went there for one second?
Me: Still die.
Isaac: What if I wore something. Rock?
Me: It would melt.
Isaac: Ice.
Me: Also melt.
Isaac: The thickest ice in the world.
Me: No.
Isaac: Plastic. Oh no plastic melts.

February 1st 2013 (Aged 6 yrs, 7 months) I ask if he knows what day it is.

Isaac: The oneth of February [pron. *wunth*]
Me: We don't say oneth.

He tries again.

Isaac: The onetht? [pron. *wunth-t*]

Feb 7th He plays truant to dodge swimming. He's messing about with superglue while I'm working. He comes up to me.

Isaac: One thing. How does the superglue not get stuck to the packet?
Me: Don't know.
Isaac: Clever.

Clever superglue, not me.

Feb 9th 'What's honeymoon?'

Me: After you get married you go on holiday for a month. Moon means month.
Isaac: I thought it means 'show your bottom.'

At the shops, he leads me past shelves full of coveted items. I ask where we're going and he says 'you'll see!'

Feb 13th Tube. Seeing a poster advertising malaria, he fired questions about the disease, how you catch it etc. I told him mosquitoes have a long spike and they dig it into you and suck up the blood. He was interested that mosquitoes use blood for 'food and drink.' He asked why the mosquitoes who carry malaria don't die of malaria. I didn't know.

Isaac: Which country is best for medicine?
Me: Switzerland, probably. Rich countries.
Isaac: What is England famous for?
Me: Railways.
Isaac: Medicine?
Me: Yes, some medicine.
Isaac: America is good for medicine.

He gave a big affirmative nod on 'America.' He always pronounces it 'Am-*airrrrr*ica.'

In West Bay to meet Rob Twigger.

Me: Does Twigger know everything?
Isaac: He must.

He addressed Rob as 'Twigger' until Rob told him to call him 'Captain.' Isaac did this once but kept forgetting.

Feb 17th 2013 In a cab from Bridport to Dorchester. We passed a hill with a circular shadow where an ancient fort would have stood. He wanted to know if the Victorians built it. I told him it was probably as old as the Egyptians. He didn't believe that. 'The stones would have weared out.' We also had a long, complicated and ultimately fruitless discussion about what a knuckle-duster was and how it protected your hands. Twigger had seen him buy a ring in Bridport and said 'what you need is a knuckleduster.'

Tube. A few days later. He painted lines across his fingers and asked me what they were. I didn't know. He bunched his fist and mimed a punch. 'Knuckleduster!' I guessed.

Feb 18th Tube. 'Can we one day go to America? No swimming.' [He's afraid of sharks]

Feb 20th 'Is there a place called *ham and cheese* in Sandwich?'

Me: How do you know about Sandwich?
Isaac: Leo went there. What about a place called *butter*?
Me: Could be.
Isaac: Leo broke his arm in Blackpool. How long does it take to go to Blackpool?
Me: Four hours by train.
Isaac: Car?
Me: Five hours.
Isaac: Plane?
Me: One hour.
Isaac: Rocket?
Me: Two minutes.

Always this pattern with travel. Times and means of conveyance are requested. He keeps asking how long it takes to get from New Zealand to Antarctica.

Feb 21st Tube. He handed me an invite to an art show at his school. 'Don't go.'

Me: Why not?
Isaac: I don't like being baby-sitted.
Me: Don't you like Kate?

He said, whispering, but with a certain clever joyfulness in his face: 'I don't like going to sleep on my own!'

Feb 22nd He asked if it's possible to surf from America to Australia.

Feb 25th (Age 6 yrs 8 months) Tube home.

Me: We've got to go home a different way today. Someone jumped under a train.
Isaac: Can I see?

On the Piccadilly line, he reads a new station name. 'Lickster Square, I'm going to call it Lickster Square.' [Leicester Square]

March 1st Tube. Isaac sees a picture of Harry Styles, the favourite singer of Flora.

Isaac: Who's that?
Me: Harry Styles. From Flora's favourite band.
Isaac: Oh. She hates them now.
Me: I thought she loved them.
Isaac: She changed.

He says these two last things – 'she hates them now' and 'she changed' – with a smiling and wide-eyed expression full of scandalised pleasure. He then explained, although I can't recall his precise words, that he felt that others had persuaded Flora to change her mind in public, but privately her adoration remained intact.

Home. I showed Isaac a birthday card from Marion to me. I made him read it then I threw it in the fire. He was furious. 'You're not supposed to do that!' He then punched me in the face.

March 2nd Bath-time. He asked about a singer who died in the bath. Whitney Houston. He thinks baths are lethal.

Isaac: Do you know Lily Allen?
Me: Yes.
Isaac: Is she dead?
Me: No. She's about 26.

Isaac: Do you know a song by Lily Allen?
Me: Yes.
Isaac: Sing it.
Me: I can't sing.

He asks how various people died. Being told 'it was old age' he says, 'I hate "old age" it's boring. I like *action* death. Like shot. Like that kind of action.'
He comes up with two requests for me.
Isaac: Two things. We should do more things. And what does a dead bison smell like?

March 6th 2013 Isaac in bathroom, brushing his teeth, talking to Celia.

Isaac: Were you alive when the Monument was built?
Celia: Of course not. It was built in about 1680.
Isaac: Do you know anyone who was alive when the Monument was built?
Celia: No. It was built about five hundred years ago.

March 7th Isaac watching cartoons. Me working.

Isaac: When you're blind can you feel with your feet what's coming?
Me: Yeah.
Isaac: How?
Me: Er ... Dunno.

Tube. He showed me a newly wobbly tooth and asked about the tooth fairy. I told him, as he half-suspected, that the coin was put under the pillow by us, not by the tooth fairy. But he was scandalised that the tooth fairy is fiction. 'You shouldn't have told me that.'

Moments later:

'How does the baby get into the mummy's tummy?'

I said 'I don't know. It's very complicated.' He said 'you do know. Tell me.'

'Oh. Look at that Isaac. In the paper. That man's eating a scorpion.'

Anything to spare me the hell of explaining reproduction on a crowded tube.

Days later, he lost a tooth & collected £5 from the tooth fairy. He didn't suggest that we'd supplied the cash. His belief in the tooth fairy seems unshakeable.

March 11th 2013 Puzzling over maths. Multiply and multiplication baffle him.

Me: Multiply is the action. Multiplication is the fact, the deed.
Isaac: I don't understand. Will I?
Me: Yes.
Isaac: At university?
Me: Yup, or possibly before.

We looked at the Highway Code before Celia failed her driving test. I suggested a game: silly meanings for the signs, e.g. the 'galloping deer' symbol.

Me: What does it mean?
Isaac: Watch out, it's Christmas.

The symbol prohibiting a U-turn, said Isaac, meant 'Huge Magnet Up Ahead.'

March 15th Tube

Isaac: What's taekwondo?
Me: Like aikido. It's a martial art.
Isaac: What's the difference?

Me: I don't know.
Isaac: Which one hurts most?
Me: I don't know. You know who would know ...

This means Robert Twigger. But instead of saying Twigger he fell silent and wouldn't say Twigger, even after my prompting.

Me: Who would know the difference?
Isaac: Of course, he would.

[refusing to say 'Twigger']

Me: Who?
Isaac: You know.
Me: All martial arts hurt. Do you want to do the one that hurts most?
Isaac: The one that hurts least.

He'd baked cakes at school and I accidentally left them on the tube. Which annoyed him. Walking home he got tired and walked slowly. I waited while he caught up. He was so cross he stopped talking. His face froze and he walked with his eyes straight ahead, not looking at me, except with a brief defiant glance.

'Isaac? You've very quiet,' I said. 'You've stopped talking to me, haven't you? OK, let's play a game. I'll see if I can make you talk, right? Yes? Can I make you talk? We'll play that game, shall we? Can I make Isaac talk? Yes or no?'

He realized that 'No' would lose him the game instantly. This made him grin. I then ran away from him and he chased me.

March 18th Tube from school.

Isaac: Do you know how to make a chatterbox?
Me: No.
Isaac: Wrong!

Me: No.
Isaac: Me. I'm a chatterbox.

March 27th (Aged 6 yrs, 9 months) Isaac trying card tricks. I take a card but drop it. It lands face down so Isaac can't see the card. 'That was a good land.'

March 28th Isaac Googling *scorpion*. He asks me to spell it. Then he says 'shall I tell you how long a scorpion can hold its breath for? Up to six days.'

March 29th Tube

Isaac: Is it illegal if you're an ordinary person and you get things and make a film and put it on television, is it illegal?
Me: No. You can do that.
Isaac: But they didn't ask you.
Me: If they didn't ask you, they may not put it on.
Isaac: How do you put a programme on television?
Me: You tell them what's in the programme and ask if they want to put it on.
Isaac: What if you lie?
Me: That helps. It's important to lie because you haven't made the programme yet so you need to tell them it's going to be brilliant even if you don't know.

March 30th I collected him from Nat and Ezra's for the first time in a year. I usually carry him on my shoulders.

Me: You don't need to go on my shoulders any more.
Isaac: You will still have to if I want. Occasionally.
Me: Occasionally. That's a good word. Do you know how to spell it?
Isaac: No. Don't even tell me.

April 2nd Waking up he asked Celia if horses can have false legs. He seemed puzzled that they couldn't.

Switzerland 5-12th April 2013. He woke up with an urgent question. 'Can a volcano blow up the whole world?'

Later. 'What's the smallest Alp?'

April 18th I showed him a gap where I'd had a tooth extracted at the front of my mouth. He was horrified and closed my mouth by putting his fingers under my jaw and snapping it upward.

Me: Don't you want to see?
Isaac: Neeeoooo!! It's still bleeding.

He has a new way of saying 'no.' ... Neeeoooooooo!

Returning from school.

Isaac: Seahorses I always knew this, I always knew this, seahorses are the only animals that the men have the babies. And they change colour when they're happy.
Me: The men or the babies?
Isaac: The seahorses. They're a bit like kangaroos. They keep the baby in the pouch.

Tube. Friday, half day. I collect him at 12.15. The District line train is heading for Wimbledon.

Isaac: Did you live in Wimbledon?
Me: Yes.
Isaac: Can we one day go there?
Me: Yes.
Isaac: Is it nice?
Me: Yes.
Isaac: Have I been there?
Me: No.

Interesting that he still places 'one day' eccentrically mid-sentence. 'Can we one day go there?' Crossing Sloane Square we saw Allegra, aged 6, waving from her mum's car.

Me: Nice car. A Mercedes.
Isaac: Jeremy has a Mercedes.
Me: That's right! Do you remember he used to have a BMW and he took you for a ride in it? When you were two. Remember?
Isaac: No.
Me: And you used to give him the car-key and say 'key' instead of 'give me a ride in the car?'
Isaac: Could I walk?
Me: Yes.
Isaac: What was my main word?
Me: 'Get it.'

I asked him if he learned anything at school. He said he watched a DVD and then did French.

Me: What did you learn in French?
Isaac: How to say my birthday.
Me: Go on. ... the 23rd June

Long pause.

Isaac: I forgot how you say 'twenty.'
Me: Vingt.
Isaac: Vingt. Yeah vingt.
Me: Twenty-three?

Long pause.

Me: Vingt-trois.
Isaac: Vingt-trois.
Me: June?
Isaac: Vingt-trois Joon.

Me: Great.
Isaac. And that's all I learned today.

I couldn't be bothered correcting 'Joon' to Juin.

April 19th We watch a livestreamed play, *The Arrest of Ai Wei Wei*.

Me: It's about an artist in China who was arrested. That's all I know.
Isaac: Maybe he painted something on the walls and he wasn't allowed.

Before the livestream, I show him *Ace of Spades* by Motorhead on YouTube. He points to Phil Taylor. 'He looks a bit like Michael Jackson. Are any of them dead?' We watch *Back in Black* by AC/DC. He's fascinated by the guitarist's school uniform. I start typing as he talks.

Isaac: How can he fit a school uniform on? Are you going to write that down?
Me: Yup.
Isaac: What!? It's a good question!

The Arrest of Ai Wei Wei begins. I ask him to be quiet. 'What if I'm dying to say something? What if I'm *really dying* to say it?' After ten minutes. 'It's very boring. They're just sitting in a room. Is anything going to happen exciting?'

Later –

'How long's the first round?' [first act]

And

'How long's it been up?' [been on]

At the end of the dull play, Ai Wei Wei starts shouting 'fuck' a lot.

Isaac: He's definitely going to jail.

April 21st 2013 Morning wake-up question. 'Can you weigh a soul?'

This was inspired by sculptures above the door of a cathedral in Berne showing the Last Judgement. I told him you couldn't weigh a soul. 'What about babies? They weigh babies!'

April 27th (Aged 6 years, 10 months) Isaac told me that after going to the Tower of London with Celia and Leo they went to a church. He said a prayer 'for your Dad' as he calls him. He lit a candle. 'It was only 50p. Sometimes it's free.'

April 28th Walking to Leo's, I told Isaac I would love to be six years old and on my way to my best friend's house.

Isaac: Did you like being a child?
Me: Yes! Nothing to do all day but muck around while the adults do all the work.
Isaac: Did your mum work a lot?
Me: Yes, she baked rock cakes and scones every day.
Isaac: Is she a home-made lady?
Me: Yes.
Isaac: I like home-made. Did she make jam?
Me: No.
Isaac: It's quite hard making jam.

May 3rd Isaac pestered me to tell him about science experiments so I explained how to make a nuclear bomb. Follow-up questions galore.

A tube ride after a party at Chelsea Harbour Club. Just me and Isaac. He asked me about more experiments. I know very little about 'experiments' so I told him how to make a nuclear bomb using two lumps of uranium, a pipe and a stick of dynamite.

'Enough to blow up a city,' I told him. He modified the design and suggested that with two smaller bits of uranium the bomb would blow up a house. I told him I wasn't sure.

'It either has to be massive or it doesn't happen at all,' I said.

He suggested using a nuclear bomb to blow up a nuclear bomb. I said that would blow up the whole world. Then:

Isaac: Who was the first person ever, before the Greeks, before the Egyptians?

He realised it was contradictory to talk about the first mummy because she had a mummy.

'Who was the first caveman?'
'We don't know.'
'Were the cavemen famous?'
'No.'

He realised this was a silly question and solemnly corrected himself, 'the cavemen didn't have famous.' After we'd been talking for ages, a blonde American, about 30, got off the train. As she left she told me she'd been listening to him (as had others.) 'You must be so proud,' she said.

Later Isaac asked me to buy him a suit like Bond's in *Skyfall* for his birthday.

May 4th Isaac trying to find Fred Astaire on YouTube. He enjoyed Fred Astaire videos when he was small and called him 'Freddy Stairs.' I told him we'd simplified the name and Isaac felt he'd been tricked. He preferred the familiar name 'Freddy Stairs' and pointed to his feet. Obvious link – stairs and dancing.

Isaac: Who's your favourite singer?
Me: Robert Plant.

Isaac: Noooo!
Me: My favourite band? Led Zeppelin.
Isaac: Don't you like, what's his name, whatsa name again, I asked you before and you said someone else. It's a boy. What's his name again?
Me: Elvis.
Isaac: Elvis. Elvis definitely hasn't met Freddy Stairs.

May 5th Pond. He found tadpoles. Then he asked if they were called 'tadpoles.' Or had he been tricked about them too?

May 6th Celia tells him about a forthcoming trip to Singapore in August, four months away.

Me: Hi Isaac. Are you going to Singapore?
Isaac: Now?

He watches a film about planets and meteors.

Isaac: What's the last planet?
Me: The furthest away? Pluto.
Isaac: Do you know what it used to be called? Planet X.

Later, he asks 'is Pluto polluted?' He pronounces Pluto 'Polluto.'

Then:

Isaac: Daddy, come. It's a meteor dip, look a meteor dip.
Me: That's a crater.

On the computer he made paintings with a semi-automatic programme. They were like Mondrians. I showed him some paintings by Cy Twombly and he couldn't believe they'd been done in earnest. He thought a baby had painted them. I showed him a photo of Cy Twombly. I said 'here's the man who did them.' Isaac: 'Is he a baby painter?'

I bought red wine in a box which fascinated him. He poured wine for anyone from 'the squeezer.' Celia wanted some and I showed Isaac how to pour it. But he felt that more ceremony was required. He insisted on placing the wine on a tray and carrying it into the sitting-room. Off he went. I foresaw disaster, involving tragic spillages, so I stopped him and removed the tray. I told him to carry the wine by hand. That was a sight – him holding the wine in two hands, one on the bulb, the other on the stem, his eyes torn between focusing on his steps or on the wine.

May 10th Garden. Isaac and Leo mucking about. Isaac kicks over my glass of wine.

Isaac: Sorry.
Me: Better get me another.
Isaac: Yes!

He celebrates this, like a slam-dunk in baseball, with a sharp downward drive of both elbows. Then he puts his hands together and prays. 'Thank you God, for making me spill the wine so I can get more from the squeezer.' Later he calls the wine-box 'the squeezy wine.'

May 11th Tube. He draws a complicated target for some kind of James Bond-related effort. Above it he writes 'Goldin Bullit.'

May 12th Leo arrives. Celia and Isaac are at a funfair. We go to find them and Leo tells me it's Seskin's birthday.

Me: How old is he?
Leo: Forty. How sad. He's getting really old.

May 14th 2013

Isaac: Can a child dye their hair?
Me: Yes.

Isaac: Dark gold?
Me: Yes. Your hair's dark gold.
Isaac: What colour is impossible to dye?
Me: No idea.
Isaac: Your own colour!

As he leaves the house. 'When I was three I wanted to meet Michael Jackson. Or four.'

May 15th Tube. Trying to read 'tough break' in a newspaper. He said 'towf – what's towf?' A familiar error.

Later he says 'in America they have those flappy pub doors. But not in New York.'

May 19th He won a box of soldiers at a fairground and played with them outside the Palm Tree while I had a pint. He knocked them all over and started holding funerals for the dead (at my suggestion, to wind up the game.) He had an idea for winning a war. The soldiers lie down pretending to be dead and then jump up and ambush the enemy. 'Is that in the rules?' he asked.

We watched Motorhead on YouTube. He sat patiently through *Ace of Spades* – for the second time.

Isaac: Which one of them's dead?
Me: None of them.
Isaac: A band and none of them's dead!

I played *Bomber* and he said 'it's getting a little bit annoying' as Lemmy roared madly into the mike.

Me: Lemmy's Welsh I think.
Isaac: The Welsh are good singers.

That's Isaac patronising me!

May 19th Tadpoles in the pond. A crowd of tadpoles clustered together.

Me: Look. Why's there a big group of them there?
Isaac: Maybe it's a concert.

May 20th 'What if you had a house made of matches and a fireplace made of matches and you lit a fire?'
Me: What do you think?
Isaac: It would explode. It would take quite a long time.

May 21st Tube home after school.

Isaac: What's s'il vous plait?
Me: It means please.
Isaac: In what language?
Me: What language? French! The language you've been learning for three years
Isaac: Oh yeah, I remember. How do I say, *please can I go to the toilet?* I know. *S'il vous plait can I go to the toilet?*

May 29th (Aged 6 yrs, 11 months) Watching a dinosaur movie, he says to me, out of nowhere. 'You know the T-Rex is not the biggest meat-eater?'

He still says 'did I fall to sleep?' and 'Ezra by mistake hit me.'

After falling asleep in the evening he woke up. As ever, fascinated by his own actions.

Isaac: Did I fall to sleep?
Me: Yes.
Isaac: How long?
Me: Ten minutes.

June 9th I ordered Isaac an electric piano. It didn't arrive. Isaac: 'I had a dream the piano came and it was made of chocolate.'

Isaac: What's your favourite money?
Me: Sterling.
Isaac: I thought you said stolen money.

At a party Isaac met a boy called Rohan.

Isaac: How old are you?
Rohan: Five.
Isaac: When are you going to be six?
Rohan: How do you know I'm going to be six?

June 11th Isaac standing in front of a mirror about to put on his pyjamas. 'My willy looks like a chicken's neck.'

Looking through a book of kings and queens.

Isaac: Was George VI very famous?
Me: Yes.
Isaac: Did he drive the Titanic?

June 15th Listening to *Swan Lake* with Isaac and Celia.

Me: This is by Tchaikovsky. He's dead.
Isaac: How did he die?
Me: Don't know. Old age?
Isaac: [disappointed] Oh.
Me: OK he was shot by the secret police while falling into a volcano.
Isaac: And writing music.
[Beat]
Isaac: Was he really?
Me: Shot by the secret police? I doubt it.
Celia: It was before the days of the secret police.
Me: No, it wasn't. The tsar had secret police. They put the secret police on Tolstoy.
Isaac: They put the secret police on Toy Story!??!!!

Later, I'm watching the news. Adele has got the MBE and they play a burst of *Someone Like You* which Isaac knows well. He's away from the TV and he turns to me with his eyes full of expectation. 'Is she dead?'

Isaac comes into the kitchen with Leo trailing behind. Isaac wants me to clear out, so he says 'bye.'

Me: What are you planning?
Isaac: Nothing.
Me: What - ?
Isaac: Writing father's day cards for our children.
Me: How many children have you got?
Isaac: Thirty.

Isaac reveals his knowledge of French.

Me: What did you learn in French this week?
Isaac: Le, la.
Me: And what does it mean?
[Long pause]
Isaac: Wait.
[Long pause]
Isaac: Female, something.
Me: It means 'the.' Le and la is masculine and feminine.
Isaac: That's right.

He explains the difference between le and la with a level of inaccuracy which is almost poetic.

Isaac: If it's le without an 'e' it's le. And if it's le with an 'e' it's la.
Me: And what does it mean?
[Long pause]
Isaac: They didn't tell us that!

This, after learning French at private schools for three years. Jesus.

Age **Seven**

June 23rd 2013 Downstairs with Roman. Isaac is strumming his new guitar, left-handed, which is odd. 'He's not playing a chord,' said Roman. I asked Isaac to mime strumming and he did it right-handed. Holding the actual guitar he played left-handed.

Me: I'll have to re-string it for you. You're left-handed. Like Paul McCartney. And Jimi Hendrix – the best guitar player of all time.

Isaac lights up, starts chanting.

'Yeahhhhhh! I'm left-handed. I'm left-handed. He's the best guitar player. I'm the best guitar player!'

Contributory factor – Roman is right-handed.

Later we take a cab to a party and pass a demonstration of Sikhs. Roman watches and announces 'the last brown one has just gone past.'

June 28th Train with Isaac. He asks me about a lady rolling a cigarette. I explain that some people make their own cigarettes.

Isaac: Did Mummy do that?
Me: No.
Isaac: Too lazy.

Isaac told me he learned something in French today – how to order in restaurants.

Me: Go on then.
Isaac: Oon hot-dog and oon Coca Cola. Is that good?

June 29th Isaac on Trash Packs. 'Shall I tell you why you have to collect them because you're meant to make up a story at the end.

Once upon a time there was a Trash Pack and the boy came walking down the street, a bit like that. Are you writing this down?'
'Yes.'
This clams him up. I asked him to name his best friend in the world.
'Leo.'
'Best friend at school?'
'Flora.'

He decided to place everyone he knows in order.
'First everyone in my family, including the ones who are dead. They all count as one person, yes?'
'OK.'

Then he did the full list but Flora was top, not Leo.

[Flora then vanishes from the record. Her parents moved to Abu Dhabi]

July 14th He's off to France. I tried to teach him easy French. 'Je voudrais un croissant.' I drummed it in several times, then tested him. He asked me for thinking time.

Me: How do you say I'd like a croissant?
Isaac: Wait ....
Me: I'd like a croissant.
Isaac: Wait ....
Me: I'd like.
Isaac: Wait ...
Me: I?
Isaac: Le?

In Devon. We go to Westward Ho! which he insists on pronouncing strangely to honour the exclamation mark. He shouts 'Ho!' but says 'Westward' at normal volume.

'Westward *HO!*'

Celia hired him a wetsuit, tight at the neck, which he said felt 'strangly.' After he learned that 'the cousins' were coming he became distracted and demanded to know when they'd arrive.

Me: Three quarters of an hour.
Isaac: Is that an hour chopped into three bits?

Aug 4th (Aged 7 yrs, 1 month) Isaac asks me about some posh trolley he saw at a posh hotel and he wonders if this posh amenity is typical of posh places.

Me: I don't go to posh places like that. I'm not posh.
Isaac: No.
Me: Are you posh?
Isaac: Bit.
Me: Is mummy posh?
Isaac: Yes.

On the phone to Isaac from Edinburgh. He said one of the builders was called Lloyd. He added that the ceiling had been removed, 'and we can see the fluff that keeps us warm' [insulation]

Aug 16th Isaac asked us about a film called *Grandfather*. We both scratched our heads. Isaac kept asking and said it was scary and had a horse's head in a bed.

'The Godfather'

He repeated it. We laughed. He said, 'what? Why's that funny?'

Isaac and Leo:

Isaac: Do you love yourself?
Leo: No.
Isaac: That means you don't like what God made.

Train to Wales. Isaac asks about his birth. 'Was I late or early?'
Celia: Late!
Isaac: What if I was late cos I didn't want to get out. What if I was being lazy?

Aug 27th (Aged 7 yrs, 2 months) After a day out with Celia, he comes into the garden to interest me in his new purchase. He has a tactic.

Isaac: Which is better, a book on earth or a book on space?
Me: Book on earth.
Isaac: Why?
Me: We know more about the earth.
Isaac: I've got a book on space. Do you want to see it?

He brings it out. It's a pop-up solar system guide with Pluto downgraded from a planet to a dwarf planet. Next day, he's worried about the strict new regime at school. Before setting off he lingers by the radiator, looking down at his chest. 'I'm worried,' he says. He has to bring the correct stationery or face detention.

Me: Oh, dear. Are you really worried?
Isaac: No.
[Beat]
Isaac: Yes!

The 'no' was pretend, to reassure me. Luckily he wasn't worried. But Celia was and she'd transferred her anxieties into him.

Aug 28th Still some odd past participles. He said 'picken' for 'picked.'

Aug 30th Walking with Isaac holding a Slush Puppy drink. He asked me how it was made. I said sugar, ice, food colouring. He suggested it had flavouring too. I conceded this. He asked if we could buy some food flavouring. I said we already had vanilla. He suggested strawberry. Finally, I twigged. He was lobbying for us to make Slush Puppies at home. I told him I'd rumbled his plan. 'Yes!' he said, triumphantly.

Isaac: What's demon sense?'
Me: I don't know.
Isaac: What's human sense?
Me: Oh, common sense!

Sept 3rd Tube to school.

Me: You know what day it is today?
Isaac: Tuesday?
Me: September 3rd. You know what happened today? The second world war started.
Isaac: Is there going to be a party?
Me: Not really.
Isaac: When did the second world war start?
Me: Today. Third of September.
Isaac: First world war?
Me: August 4th. Next year, it'll be 100 years since it started.

He asked about 'the celebrations.'

Me: Well, no it's a bit sad because millions died.
Isaac: Will it be in church?
Me: Yes.
Isaac: Will you go?
Me: No.
Isaac: You won't go. ... Am I a Catholic? I'm a Catholic.
Me: You're a Protestant.
Isaac: What's that thing when you don't believe in God?
Me: Agnostic. Or atheist. That's me. I'm not sure.
Isaac: I might believe in God or I might not. I'm not sure.

He tells me that Delta, the name of his class, is Greek for D. He says ancient Greek is an option for older kids among other possible subjects.

Isaac: It's a choice.
Me: What's the choice?
Isaac: To learn it or not to learn it.

He asked what's 'the best thing to learn', i e. the most useful. Good question. Then he told me about his spelling test tomorrow in French. He'll be tested on salut, bonjour and bon soir. He said salut looks like salt.

Me: Do you know how to say 'hi boss' in French?
Isaac: How?
Me: Salut chef.

I suggested that he say 'salut chef' to his French teacher who would find it funny.

Isaac: How do you say OK?
Me: D'accord.
Isaac: D'accord chef. OK boss.

He said he'd say that to his French teacher. Then he said that 'd'accord chef' should be the name of our band. He said older boys had lockers.

Isaac: Did you have a locker at school?
Me: Yes.
Isaac: How old?
Me: When I was 13. I think I had one when I was younger as well, when I was nine.

He asked if I had a locker 'at secondary school' – (first use of that phrase) – and if I had a locker 'at university'?

Sept 9th 2013 Isaac at home. I needed to watch our Toshiba TV to write a parliamentary sketch. We call it 'Toshiba' as if it's a person.

Isaac: Can I watch Toshiba?
Me: For three quarters of an hour.
Isaac: That's nearly an hour!

Later

Isaac: Who wrote Harry Potter?
Me: JK Rowling.
Isaac: Where?
Me: Edinburgh. In a café in Edinburgh.
Isaac: Who for?
Me: She had a child and all she wanted to do was to earn enough to feed the child.
Isaac: Was she poor?
Me: Yes.
Isaac: How could she afford paper?

Tube. Lots of questions about decades.

'Were you alive in the 80s?'
'Yes.'
'The 20s?'
'No. Grandma was.'
'Your dad?'
'Yes. Just.'
'Your great-grandfather?'
'Yes.'
'Great-great-grandfather?'
'No.'
'He was alive before. What are we in now?'
'Well the first decades of the century don't really have names. In seven years it'll be the 20s. The 2020s.'

'How old will you be?'
'Work it out, Isaac.'
[Much muttering]
'57.'
'Yes.'
'How old will Mummy be?'
'Work it out.'
[More muttering]
'50.'
'Yes.'
'And how old will I be?'
'Work it out.'
[A surprising amount of muttering]
'14.'

At home, I looked at his Science experiment book. It showed 'observations' recorded by him after simple actions like dissolving a sugar lump in drops of water. He put vinegar onto bicarb and saw it bubble and hiss. He's been told to list the observations as follows:

What we see
What we hear
What we smell
What we touch

But not

What we taste

A safety-conscious school! He told me he'd asked his science teacher what plutonium was. The teacher had laughed.

At home after his bath he told me about practising javelin. He said the class had split along gender lines with the boys signaling 'thumbs downs' and chanting 'down with the girls!' He showed me the gestures. And he asked if that was funny. Then he said 'how do you javel?' He thought 'javeling' was a verb from 'to javel.' He demonstrated his action. He seems to be left-handed in that sport although it's not certain. He's like me. Right hand, left hand. A bit of this, a bit of that.

Sept 11th 2013 Isaac at home, sick. Sitting with the laptop, cross-legged in his light blue stripey pyjamas, he does an almighty sneeze over the keyboard. He curls forward & tries to wipe it with the shirt-tails of his pyjama top, still cross-legged.

Me: Did you do snot on the computer?
Isaac: A lot! Not snot but spit. I'm not cleaning it. I'm going upstairs to have a rest. My tummy hurts.

To avoid school he grades his health each morning using the star system. If he's not quite right he says 'half a star.' If he's feeling OK he gives himself 'a quarter star.' If he's fine he draws a big circle in the air – meaning no stars.

Isaac watching *Chitty Chitty Bang Bang.* He reads out the credits and asks me if I recognise the actors. My friend Melinda's dad, Ken Hughes, is the director so when the name appears he reads it out. 'Ken Hudgees Hudgees Ken Hudgees – is it your friend's dad?'

Sept 21st Leo and Isaac playing schools.

Isaac: What are we doing?
Leo: We're identifying. Do you know what identify means?
Isaac: Indentify?*
Leo: Indentify, yes. It means 'investigate.'

[I call out]

Me: It means 'name.'
Leo: It means 'find out.' My teacher said.
Me: He meant 'find out the name.'

Leo: I will cut him in half.

[*Isaac misheard identify as indentify and Leo copied the error]

Sept 26th 2013 (Aged 7 yrs, 3 months) Isaac was asked at school to name the 'occupation' of his parents – a new word. One girl's mum worked at the *Storm* model agency. On the tube, in the newspaper, I showed him an advert of a man in a suit. I said he was a photographic model.

Isaac: What if he shakes?
Me: Why?
Isaac: Needs the loo.

Later, talking about weddings, I mentioned that ours was in St Mary Undercroft, beneath the houses of parliament.

'I got married underground,' I told him.
'Like Hitler,' he said.

When he looks at a photo of any celeb, he asks if it's a modeling photo.

Oct 3rd Isaac has learned that he's at a private school. He's puzzled & wonders if it means a school that's secret. He showed me his class photo which includes an enormous boy who looks about 16. 'That's Alexander. He can't spell his name.'

He likes his new friend Evan even more than Billy. He demonstrates how much more by holding thumb and forefinger half an inch apart. This conflict of loyalties worries him. He says 'that's Evan's car.' And he points out that he just said 'Evans.' He likes that and tells me he likes it.

Oct 8th Reading through sheet music he mispronounces 'Odd to Joe.' [Ode to Joy]

Kate, next door, came over. We had a bowl of plums and I told Isaac to go in and present them to Celia and Kate and to say 'ladies, plums are served.' He nearly made it but said: 'Plums are being served.'

Me watching TV and Isaac listening. The show is about a British revolt against the Romans. 'Are they talking about Nero?' he said. Doing a project on Nero, he hears Boudicca mentioned.

Isaac: Was she the only lady emperor?

Later

Isaac: Boudicca died from being stabbed.

Oct 25th 2013 (Aged 7 yrs, 8 months) The difference between diamond and metal. He knows metals are hard but he wonders why diamond, the hardest substance, can't be worked or turned into ingots.

Isaac: What's the hardest metal?
Me: Steel. It was discovered by accident.
Isaac: Yes, I discover things by accident.

Nov 1st Imperial War Museum. Isaac asks about distances. 'Is there such a thing as kilo-miles?'

Outside, huge guns. He stands next to shells nearly as big as he is. He hugs them and leans his head against them. He wants me to photograph him hugging the shells and asks if they're bullets or bombs. Inside, he finds a new row of shells, differently coloured. He hugs these and asks me which is my favourite. I say I don't care because I dislike shells. But he asks and asks. Eventually I say 'the grey one.' He says 'apart from the grey one.' I say 'all right the yellow one.' He says 'and apart from the yellow one.' I say 'the black one.' This is incredibly important to him: what is my favourite shell. I don't like this much. He sees a pillion bike. 'What do you call a motorbike with one person driving and one person not driving?'

On the train he reads 'wafer' in an advert. He pronounces it 'worr-fuh' on the analogy of 'water.' There's a single letter's difference. Water. Wafer. They should be pronounced the same way. Fair enough.

Nov 4th 2013 Outside school.

Isaac: When did the best actor in the world die?
Me: 1989. [Olivier]
Isaac: How old were you?
Me: 26.
Isaac: How old was he?
Me: 82.
Isaac: Who's the worst actor who's an actor?

Nov 10th Isaac mucking about as Celia tries to put his clothes on.

Celia: Adults get fed up with children being naughty.
Isaac: Well, I get fed up with adults being naughty.

Nov 11th Home from school. Pain in his ear. 'I've got a really really really really really really really really really – infinity reallys – bad ear.'

Nov 12th Morning. Celia and Isaac.

Celia: Have you seen Leo when he passes a mirror, he goes like this. He can't stop looking at himself.
Isaac: That's what you do Mummy. He's copying you.

Later Celia talks to me.
Celia: Apparently everyone at school had to think of an adjective to describe Isaac.
Me: What did they say?
Isaac: Noisy. Scruffy. Sweet.

Nov 21st Isaac watching Paul McCartney being interviewed. Sir Paul!

Isaac: Is Paul McCartney married?
Me: Yes.
Isaac: What's his wife called?
Me: Lady McCartney.
Isaac: Did her parents call her Lady?

By the sitting-room fire. Cellar door open. Isaac told me to close it. He'd watched a zombie film and was scared of zombies rising up from the cellar. He was serious.

Nov 24th (Aged 7 yrs, 5 months) Me, Isaac & Celia discussing Isaac's potential as a barrister.

Me: Do you want to be a barrister?
Isaac: What's a barrister?
Me: You know, a lawyer, where Mummy works, wearing a wig.
Isaac: Do they have a hammer?

Isaac takes the red Bible from my room. In dumb-show he points to the title, *Holy Bible*. I ask if he's doing 'church.' He nods silently and goes to his room. Later I overhear this in a loud, public voice:

'Thank you for the stuff you've given us. Thank you for creating earth. Thank you for letting all the children and all the adults become friends. And look after the people who have gone to heaven from earth. Look after them. Right.'

I went in. He was dressed in a red velvet cape and swimming goggles. I left. A few minutes later, I heard a lot of machine-gun fire.

Isaac fears being poisoned by toxic smoke from the fireplace. If I throw in a bit of plastic, he thinks he's about to die and approaches the fire gingerly, monitoring the smoke, with one hand clamped over his mouth and the other hand over his heart in case it stops beating.

Dec 5th Tube. Isaac and me in a crowd of commuters.

Isaac: How old were you when Elvis died?
Me: 13. No, 14.
Isaac: Was he on the television – that he died?
Me: Yes.
Isaac: How old was he when he was a singer?
Me: When he started?
Isaac: Yes.
Me: 20 or 21.
Isaac: When?
Me: 1956.
Isaac: I thought it was 1957.
Me: Oh, all right, 1957.

This got a peal of laughter from a woman standing next to Isaac, i.e. right above his head.
Isaac writes to Santa. 'Shall I write Dear Santa Claus or do it the American way and write Santa?' He writes it and asks me for the postcode of the hotel we'll be staying at on Christmas Eve. He's curious about my childhood.

Isaac: Did you write a letter to Santa?
Me: No.
Isaac: Didn't you get any presents?
Me: Yes.
Isaac: Strange!

He's baffled. Then he suggests that my parents bought the presents. He believes that not all presents come from Santa, some come from parents. Then we discuss Santa being like God because not everyone believes in him. 'Who designed what he looks like?'

He orders an 'obot' from Santa – a cleaning robot, costing a thousand pounds. 'Santa can make it.' Later. 'Where's Lapland? How far it is? How long would it take to get there?'

I show him a heavily airbrushed photo of Julie Andrews, aged 78, and ask him to guess her age. Isaac: 'Twenty. No, forty.'

Dec 16th Isaac in his bedroom. Celia says 'let's go and get the Christmas tree.' He's busy.

Isaac: I'm getting the baddies ready for war.

He asks me to help him Sellotape a big chunk of Lego horizontally onto his shelf. I manage it and he wants to add another chunk. I tell him it's impossible. He succeeds. He berates me. 'I did it. It's not impossible.'

Me: Well done.
Isaac: I did something impossible. Give me a hundred pounds for doing something impossible.

Dec 17th 2013 Isaac studies instructions for card tricks. 'What's exer mine?' [he pronounces it, 'x uh mine.']

Me: Examine.

Dec 18th 'I'm bored with magic. I wish you had a different job. One day I'm just going to ask your boss to fire you.'
Dec 24th 2013 (Aged 7 yrs, 6 months) Exeter. Questions in a restaurant.

Isaac: Who invented paper? Who invented bread? Who killed Shakespeare?
Me: He wasn't killed.
Isaac: How did he die? Maybe he died of writing. Maybe he died of the night shift.

More questions. 'Who was Attila the Hunt?'

Isaac: I know what a thermometer is full of.
Me: What?
Isaac: Mars. Bits of Mars. [Mercury]

Dec 28th Entering the lift in the Exeter hotel. 'You can never tell the time. Because the seconds go past.'

[Could be one of Zeno's paradoxes]

London. After long tussles and much recrimination, I settle down with Isaac to play burning bits of plastic in the fire. I throw in a plastic bottle which, according to his teacher, is something you should never do. And Isaac wants to play *Would I Lie To You?* I'm reluctant.

He screams. 'You are the stupidest, dumbest, horriblest person ever! Now play with me!!!'

I told him this was a contradiction and he laughed.

Dec 31st Isaac at breakfast with what appears to be a new teddy bear.

Me: Is that a new bear?
Isaac: No. Builder Bear I got it last year.
Me: I thought you were too old for bears.
Isaac: No! [said with smiling indignation]

I asked what 'Builder Bear' is.

Isaac: Builder Bear is when you get it and you're allowed to stuff it yourself.
Me: Oh. *Build A Bear.*

We watch a documentary about a balloon trip over Mt Everest. The balloon takes off and there's a close-up of the expedition leader, on the ground, watching the rising balloon and reciting a poem and a prayer and wishing them luck, half-fearing they're about to die. He weeps and lowers his head.

Isaac: Did you see his fillings. Have you got fillings like that?
Me: Oh, Isaac! You should be concentrating on what he said, not his teeth. That was really emotional.
Isaac: What's emotional?
Me: Feelings.
Isaac: I said – his fillings. Have you got fillings like that?

[feelings/fillings]

Jan 9th 2014 Celia says to me, 'you need a marriage counsellor.'
Isaac: 'What's a marriage canceller?'

Jan 10th Tube entrance. An old chap with a magnificently wrinkled face is slumped against the doorway, wrapped in a brown overcoat, clutching a can of Special Brew. Isaac whispers to me.

Isaac: Did you see him? That's the tramp.
Me: And Mummy gave him some money?
Isaac: Yes.
Me: How much?
Isaac: Three pounds. He's Irish.

Then Isaac, as if on a quite unrelated topic, asks 'do you have bad genes, your family?'

I mention this to Celia later. And she says, 'oh I think that's all right.' Which it is.

Jan 12th I prepared to visit Aberystwyth alone. Isaac feared I might be hit by the waves ravaging the seafront. I told him I'd be fine and then I teased him and said I might be hit by a huge wave with a shark in it. He got really upset and started crying (it was late and he was in bed.)

Next day, long train delays. I phoned him at 5.30 pm and said I was still in England (just outside Shrewsbury) not Wales. 'But Wales is in England,' pronounced the great cartographer.

Back home. I asked Isaac about his horse-riding club and if he knew anyone in the club.

Isaac: Jack. But I scarcely know him.

I gave Isaac look that said '*scarcely* – that's a new word.'

Isaac: I've said it before.
Me: How many times?
Isaac: About three.

I tried a joke. 'What word have you only said three times?' He got it. 'Scarcely' may mean 'only three times.' He found it funny.

Me: What letter comes after X in the alphabet?
Isaac: Y.
Me: I don't know. It just does.

Jan 19th I asked what he wants to be when he grows up.

Isaac: RAF. What's that again?
Me: Royal Air Force. You want to join the RAF?
Isaac: Or be a scientist. Or be the boss of the Bank of England. Do you get a lot of money?
Me: Yeah.
Isaac: Eight grand?
Me: More.
Isaac: Nine hundred thousand?
Me: Not quite.

Going to Leo's, Isaac asks what language 'Leo' is.

Me: Latin. A lot of popes were called Leo.
Isaac: After what do you get a new pope?
Me: After the old one dies, although the last one just resigned.
Isaac: Can you do that?
Me: Looks like it. He did.
Isaac: What is the pope?
Me: Head of the Catholic church.
Isaac: What's the Catholic church?
Me: Well, it was started by Jesus.
Isaac: So he was the pope.
Me: No. St Peter was the first pope.
Isaac: Of the whole world?
Me: Yup.

We walk on. I'm wearing dark glasses.

Isaac: You look like you're blind. Why do blind people wear dark glasses?
Me: I don't know. Actually, yes, because some sand or grit might blow into their eyes but they can't see it. So they wear dark glasses.
Isaac: Why did you say "I don't know"?
Me: Because I didn't know. I'd never thought about it. So I worked it out.
Isaac: Was that a good question?
Me: Very good. Do you want ten pounds?
Isaac: Yes. Give me ten pounds!

Jan 21st 2014 Isaac at home. He performs a communion service with an altar on a towel sprinkled with talcum powder and spread with 'holy keys' and 'holy crosses' and a candle in a glass and three tall glasses of water. He invents a liturgy and turns to me for questions. His 'service' includes a reference to the problematic question of hell which I'd discussed with him. God created hell, I told him, but he may not have sent anyone there.

Isaac begins. 'We will now sprinkle ...' and he chucks bits of herbs into the candle and mutters 'Dear God.'

Isaac: We're now about to eat Jesus's body and Jesus's blood. Don't you think it's a bit mean? Wait, what are those people called who eat other people?
Me: Cannibals.
Isaac: You know when they say eating Jesus's body, do they mean it?
Me: Suppose so.
Isaac: That's why I think it's a bit silly.

He gives me 'wine' which is water and 'communion' i.e. herbs. After half an hour, during which he scatters great puffs of talcum powder everywhere, he finishes the service by blowing out the candle. 'We will now send God off to his own business.'

Later, another service with a big walking stick. Isaac mounts a chair. Preaches.

Isaac: Everyone knows God. God is the most powerful and famous person. Jesus was alive. He was walking upon us. But Jesus never was. He was crucified and if he wasn't he wouldn't be here. Amen. We all know God. Who is God? God is the best. Jesus is the best. God never walked upon us, never walked on earth, Jesus did. But he is still in the clouds and heaven. Someone has never gone to hell. But someone might have. We do not know what hell and heaven look like. We will now collect the money for this church and charity and God.

Hammers on floor with the walking stick and goes round with a magician's pouch collecting from the congregation. Back on chair.

Isaac: It is now the Holy Bible. We will now read the Holy Bible. Please get out the Holy Bible from the desk where it is and please do not steal our Holy Bibles thank you.

Blows his nose. Picks up Bible.

Isaac: We will now open to page. Doesn't say the pages. Oh my God. OK. Chapter, the chapter Luke. Open to the page now please.

Hammers on floor. Reads from Bible.

Isaac: One. We are going up to five. In as much as many have undertaken to pile a narrow tive of the king, things which have been accomplished among us. 2. Just as they would delied to us by those who from the beginning were eye witness and ministers of the world. 3. Exceed God by also having followed all things closely afford some time past to write an orderly account for you most ex, excellent. 4. That you may know the truth concerning of which you have been informed.

Puts Bible down.

Isaac: Amen.

Hammers on floor.

Isaac: Finished. We will now pray. We will say how far God and Mary travelled. We will have a song first about the journey to Jerusalem.

Plays electric piano and sings. Then turns on YouTube and dances.

Isaac: Look Daddy, in church. Like this.

He puts Sammy Hagar on YouTube, *This Planet's On Fire*, and plays air-guitar with the prop that formerly served as the crucifix.

Isaac: Look Daddy, in church, I've turned the cross into a guitar.

Feb 5th 2014 (Aged 7 yrs, 7 months)

Isaac: Is coal expensive?
Me: Yes.
Isaac: Why?
Me: Because you have to go half a mile underground and dig it out.
Isaac: And by mistake you might meet lava.

Feb 15th Mile End tube, heading to Aberystwyth, Celia decides to explain the Holocaust to Isaac. She's reading a book by a Hungarian who died at Auschwitz, beaten to death, oddly enough. She mentions this to me and Isaac is immediately captivated & wants to hear the rest.

Isaac: Why, why was he beaten to death?
Celia: He was Jewish.
Isaac: What's a Jewish? Is Nuala a Jewish?

Feb 17th Aberystwyth. Isaac wanted to buy healing crystals to make Grandma better. I told him he could buy them in London. 'Where in London?'

Me: Anywhere.
Isaac: A fish shop?
Me: No.
Isaac: You said 'anywhere.'
On seeing Grandma, ill, in bed in the care-home. 'It's like she's empty. There's nothing left in her.'

Questions. In the Spanish wine-bar he asked me what were the chances of getting a Welsh newspaper, like the Western Mail, in Japan.

On the way back, passing Dovey Junction, he spotted a little bridge carrying the branch line up to Aberdovey. He asked what would happen if we went on a train over that bridge and it collapsed into the river and we had to swim away. 'How deep would it be?'

Feb 21st Collecting Isaac after a day with Bertie Banks. The mum, Loretta, repeated Isaac's questions. 'What's that block of flats? Who lives there? How much do they cost? What's communism?' She predicted that he might become a lecturer (?) Homeward bound I got more questions from Isaac. 'Did people live under London Bridge in the old days? What kind of army didn't let people go out at night and shot them if they did?'

He turned to Jack the Ripper.

Isaac: Were ladies not allowed out in the evening when Jack the Ripper was around?
Me: It wasn't that they weren't allowed. They chose not to go out. Imagine if a madman was going around killing seven-year-old boys, would you go out or stay in?
Isaac: I'd go out – for revenge with my little knife!

He told me about Bertie's strange family arrangements. 'The Dad lives in Number 40 and the Mum lives in Number 39.' Adjoining flats, separate homes.

Feb 27th **(Aged 7 yrs, 8 months)** On the way to Nuala's funeral.

Isaac: Why don't I wear a top saying *Poor Nuala*?
Me: Are you wearing your Churchill coat?
Isaac: I'm going to get my tommy gun, dagadagadagadaga, and put everyone in the box. You know which box I mean.

March 5th Tube home. Talking about communism and universal equality, he asked me what it would mean in practice. He answered this himself. 'Everyone would have the same surname.' [Almost! Communist countries give everyone the same first name – *Comrade*]

March 7th New question, oft repeated. 'When did our family start?' He got no joy from any adults on this. He even asked Jo, his cousin.

March 8th Celia makes taramasalata on toast.

Me: I like anything on toast.
Isaac: Poisonous?
Me: What?
Isaac: On toast. You said you like anything on toast. Poisonous on toast?
Me: Poison. You mean. OK, I don't like poison on toast.

March 9th Isaac in bed, near sleep, after a long day with Roman and Violet. 'When was heroin invented?' he says. I said it was refined from opium about 100 years ago (which may be right).

Isaac: What does it taste like?

March 15th Isaac runs around with Bertie singing 'everything is made of poo, if you think about it.'

Bertie's epic journey across London from Battersea on board two buses and a taxi. He counted all the CCTV cameras. He got to 790 by Liverpool Street station.

March 16th Isaac: 'How many maths words are there in the world?'

Me: What's a maths word?
Isaac: Plus. Minus. One? Is that a maths word?

For simplicity's sake I said 'there aren't that many maths words. Plus, minus, multiplied by, divided by. That's all.' He asked: 'How many literacy words are there in the world?' I said 'millions.'
March 11th Talking about Beethoven in the bath. 'Why did he go deaf? From the music? He told me he'd asked that question in the hope that I'd write it down later. He quizzed me in detail about whether I would or not.

March 14th Isaac leaving for school, Celia muttering about being late. This fascinates Isaac. 'We're late. Come on!'

Isaac: How late?
Celia: Really late.
Isaac: Ten minutes?
Celia: I don't like to think.
Isaac: Are we actually going to be late for school?
[Out they go]

March 17th Isaac with hot pink cheeks, in bed.

Isaac: I feel like – what do you call those things you put clay in?
Me: Kiln.
Isaac: Kiln. I could actually be a kiln. Put it in my mouth.

[thermometer]

April 12th (Aged 7 yrs, 9 months) By phone from Singapore, Isaac tells me that Thomas, Sarah Hurley's boy, didn't realise he'd moved to Singapore. Thomas thought it was a holiday.

'I asked him how long he'd been here and he said, a lonnnngggg time.'

Isaac told Thomas he now lived in Singapore. Thomas didn't believe this. 'Do you go to school on holiday?' asked Isaac. And the penny dropped.

April 20th Back from Singapore. Bite-marks on Isaac's arm. He said he'd been bitten everywhere. 'I'm like a mosquito smoothie.'

May 7th (Aged 7, yrs 10 months) Isaac keen on football. Asks me when Liverpool played, when Arsenal played, and a team whose name he couldn't recall.

Isaac: Diamond Mansions?

Me: Crystal Palace.

May 9th Isaac's new ploy is to 'ignore' me when he's cross. He does this on the tube and manages to hold out for 30 minutes. He explains the stratagem to me.

Isaac: Sometimes you say you're going to ignore someone. And then you want to tell the person you're ignoring something. And then you're bursting to tell them and you have to hold it in and hold it in and then you can't and you tell them.

May15th 2014

Isaac: How long's a Marathon?
Me: Twenty-six miles. From the battle of Marathon.
Isaac: They had a battle during the Marathon?

After school I took him to Trotters.

Isaac: See that old lady? She's the school nurse.
Me: You shouldn't say she's old.
Isaac: She's very kind.
Me: But which is more important, if you're a woman: to look kind or to look young?
Isaac: To look ugly.

He found this funny. Next day he was doing an experiment involving mung beans left in a dish of shallow water while they sprouted. He had to write observations.

Me: You know what science this is? Botany.
Isaac: Bottomy!

Gales of laughter.

May 22nd Chelsea Flower Show. At Susannah's display.

'Susannah had a cactus. And I touched it. But it didn't hurt.'

He was leafleting for Susannah's show. A woman asked if he was being paid. He said he wasn't – hoping she might give him some money. She didn't. This outraged him.

May 23rd (Aged 7 yrs, 11 months) Questions about plutonium, what colour is it, have I ever seen a nuclear bomb, etc. Outside the tube he notices a box of free magazines 'TNT.' He's excited and delivers a long paragraph of speculation about the magazine that Jeremy writes for, Style, in the Sunday Times, which contains 'a example' [sample] of face-cream for readers to experiment with.

Isaac: Does TNT have a example of TNT?

He hoped that TNT magazine might give away samples of explosives.

Isaac: Are you going to put that on your computer?
Me: Yes.
Isaac: Yayyyy!

May 25th Isaac doing science experiments for homework with a dummy in his mouth.

Me: Isaac, take your dummy out. Have you ever seen a scientist with a dummy?
Isaac: Yes. Me.

Isaac makes a cake. He's very keen and does it unaided.

Me: Are you going to be a baker?
Isaac: I've got a lot of decisions.

[decisions – 'options in life'] Later, I ask if he's cleaned the kitchen.
Isaac: That's your job. I made the cake. You clean up. It's fair.

I remove the cakes from the oven and he decorates them. They're good.

Me: We should start selling them.
Isaac: We'd have to get a food-tester.
Me: Right.
Isaac: But what's the point of having a food-tester because you'd just poison them after?

He assumes that the purpose of selling cakes is mass-murder.

June 9th Isaac tells me all raw meat is poisonous except chicken.

Isaac: Is the oldest building in the world a cave?
Me: Yes, although it's not really a building because no one built it.
Isaac: Oh! So that's why they're called build – dings.

June 22nd I'm talking to Coco on Whitstable beach. Coco's mother, Angel, speaks Italian.

Me: Can you speak Italian? Parlei Italiano?
Coco: A little bit.
Me: Pocito.
Coco: What?

Age **Eight**

June 28th (Aged 8 yrs, 0 months)

Isaac: Which is higher, general or admiral?
Me: Same. One's the army, the other's the navy.
Isaac: Are they basically the highest?
Me: Yes.
Isaac: Was your mum alive on the Coronation?
Me: Yes.
Isaac: How old was she?
Me: 27.
Isaac: How old was the Queen when she got her coronation?
Me: Same age.
Isaac: As who?
Me: My mum.
Isaac: Oh. So when your mum was born *she* was born, basically. [The Queen]

[Continuing]

Isaac: Is the Loch Ness basically mountains? Are there mountains around Loch Ness? Did you know Algy's father would rather have been in jail then in the war? What would you have rather done?
Me: Depends on the war.
Isaac: Second world war?
Me: War.
Isaac: I'd rather have been in jail. You wouldn't have been shot. You would have been fed. You know your grandfather went to jail. Is the jail he went to a museum?

My grandfather was a conscientious objector during WW1.]

Me: That jail is still a jail.

Isaac: If there's another world war will everyone have to join the war, over 18?

This was after Algy's pizza party. Algy's dad is a barefoot Marathon runner.

Me: Did you tell Algy your great-grandfather went to jail in the war?
Isaac: Yes. Because we made all hats, you know, in Pizza Express they give you hats, they're in the shape of second world war hats.

July 2nd Celia tells Isaac that other parents think he's erudite. He says, 'sounds like I've got lots of air. Airudite. Sounds like a disease.'

July 11th Isaac is interested in 'theory' as mentioned in his school report. I said a theory was something that may be a fact but wasn't definite.

Isaac: Is it theory or is it definite that numbers never end?
Me: Pretty much definite.
Isaac: Why?
Me: It's self-evident. It's obvious.
Isaac: It's not that obvious because we haven't counted all the numbers.

Isaac asks me to compare Roman and Leo. I decline – so he does it for me. Leo gets his preference. 'He's cleverer, he can read more, and do more sums, and he doesn't lie as much.'

July 12th Isaac: 'What's a good dog name, Mummy? ... Roger.'

July 14th Isaac watches the World Cup final on iPlayer, already aware that Germany has won.

Isaac: Do all the German people have to be from Germany?
Me: Yes.
Isaac: Be from Germany?

Me: Yes.
Isaac: Oh.
Me: Why?
Isaac: I wanted to play for them. I could do a German accent.

Later.

Isaac: Has England ever won the world cup?
Me: Once. In 1966.
Isaac: You were three.
Me: Yes.
Isaac: Were you happy?

July 19th With Isaac and diabetic Bertie at Farnborough Air Show. On the way there, Isaac tried to impress Bertie by asking me to tell him that my dad nearly got hit by a V2 rocket. Bertie listens impassively and as I finish the tale he asks me 'nuclear?'

Bertie knows a lot about 'chain guns' [machine-guns, perhaps] He tells us 'if chain guns had been invented earlier the war would probably have been a draw.'

Bertie reacts to all new information by insisting it's not new to him. A Vulcan took off at the air show and did some twirls. Isaac asked me if it was 'a bomber or a shooter.' I said 'a bomber.' I added that it probably carried a nuclear payload. Isaac told Bertie this.

Bertie: I knew it had nuclear bombs.
Isaac: When?
Bertie: I always knew it had nuclear bombs.

When the biplanes were doing near-miss stunts, Isaac and I were amazed. Two planes would hurtle towards each other at 200 mph and swerve apart at the last minute.

Me: That's so close!

Isaac: Oh my God! Did you see that?
Me: Inches apart!
Bertie: I think they were four metres apart.

Later.

Isaac: That was one of the best days of my life.
Me: What was the best?
Isaac: Legoland.
Me: Oh.
Isaac: Still it's good that it was second best.

July 22nd Questions: 'Have you heard of Bluebird? It was a racing car. It crashed into a pond.' And 'is the river Thames man-made?'

July 23rd (Aged 8 yrs, 1 month) He sees Poems on the Underground and thinks they're poems about the Underground. Fair enough. 'On' can mean 'about.' *On Melancholy.*

July 24th Isaac tells me that Bertie 'confessed' to him that he didn't like to be wrong. Bertie also claimed, when challenged over his omniscience, 'I use my common sense.'

Isaac to me, in bed. 'Do the Germans have a nuclear bomb?

Me: No.
Isaac: Ever?
Me: No, they're not allowed to have bombs.
Isaac: Why?
Me: Well last time they had lots of bombs they invaded the whole of Europe.
Isaac: Was that the second world war?
Me: Yes.

He steeples his hands and adopts a shrewd look.

Isaac: They didn't use it very wisely.

I laugh.

Isaac: Are you going to put that on your computer?
Me: Yes.
Isaac: It's their bomb, it's their responsibility.

Isaac thinks that's very funny.

Aug 1st 'You know a beaver in one year can chew through a hundred trees.'

Aug 4th He asks me how my mother died. 'I don't know,' I said, 'I didn't see her death certificate.'
Isaac: Oh, you win a certificate for being dead!

Aug 27th (Aged 8 yrs, 2 months) Back from Morocco. He told me he picked something up in the soukh and asked 'how much?' but decided against buying it. Then he got shouted at and chased down the street by the trader. Which he found odd. They stayed with Susannah's gay uncle, Andrew, at his Moroccan ranch. Isaac said the cuisine lacked variety. 'For starters, it's always, always, always, always, always, ALWAYS soup, except sometimes it isn't.'

On flying. Before take-off he makes the sign of the cross which he learned from Leo. Just the sign. He doesn't do the words although he knows them. 'On an aeroplane I always do this. And it works!'

After a long chat, he was asking silly questions like 'what's your favourite farm?' I said 'OK. Five more questions.'

Isaac: No! Thousands.

Aug 28th I explained the facts of life to him sitting in 'our spot' by the Palm Tree. I asked where the baby comes out. He pointed to his bottom.

Me: No. From the vagina.

Isaac: M'china?
Me: No, vagina.
Isaac: Front bottom.
Me: Yes and the daddy puts his willy into that. And that's how it starts.
Isaac: That's disgusting. How long for? Five minutes?
Me: Maybe.
Isaac: And you're just waiting. And reading a magazine?
Me: It can happen.

Sept 18th Isaac learning about the Celts at school. He knows he's partly Celtic and partly Anglo-Saxon. He also knows that 'barbarians' were people who had beards and that I once had a beard (from photos.) All this goes into his question.

Isaac: Am I a barbarian?
Me: No.
Isaac: Because I haven't got an axe?

Sept 28th (Aged 8 yrs, 3 months) At 'our spot' outside the pub. An old bloke in a motorised wheelchair is playing Irish ballads. Isaac asks if my mum went to the pub when I was in Ireland with her. I said yes. He asked where I was when she was in the pub. I realised that she didn't go to the pub in Ireland. The old man finished his beer and drank from a bottle of clear liquid.

Isaac: Vodka?
Me: Maybe. Vodka is Russian for water.
Isaac: It comes out of the tap!!
Me: And whisky is Irish for water.
Isaac: It comes out of the tap!!
Me: Water of life.
Isaac: Did your dad like whisky?
Me: No, beer and wine.
Isaac: Your mum?

Me: No.
Isaac: You?
Me: No.
Isaac: You're a lot like your parents. He doesn't like whisky, she doesn't like whisky.

I started laughing.

Isaac: Why's that funny?
Me: 'You're a lot like your parents' is the kind of thing an older person would say not an eight-year-old.
Isaac: I was thinking that before I said it. It's the kind of thing your uncle would say. Are you going to write that down on your computer?
Me: Yes.

Oct 5th Isaac and Roman come over with Coco. They produce a bug show with a written script. Verbatim script (mistakes included.)

Isaac: hi and wellcome to the show of insects.
Roman: today we will be telling you loads of fun facts about insects.
Coco: Bring in insects city.
Isaac: This is are bug collection. We'v been bizy collecting bugs of all diffrent sizes and tipes.
Roman: Would you look at it.
Coco: The red bin is banish bin.
Isaac: Please do not touch.
Roman: I will now read all the 18 bugs names.

HE READS ALL NAMES

[Isaac added notes to the script]

Fact 1 All worms can not live without soil
Fact 2 All wood lise eat Rotten wood

Fact 2 centerpides eat wood lise so do milerpides
Fact 3 worms cannot go fast under soil

Later, Coco finds me typing in my room and asks what I'm doing.

Me: Working, I write for a magazine.
Coco: I don't like magazines. They're boring.

Later, I'm crossing the road with her to join Isaac and Roman in the park.

Me: Who do you like best out of me, Celia and Isaac?
Coco: And Roman.
Me: And Roman.
Coco: Roman. Isaac second best, then Celia. And you're last.

She finds it hilarious that I'm last. So do I. Later I take her to a fair in Victoria Park to join the others. It's dark and from a distance we see the glow of the fair. Coco: 'It's all light-y up.'

Isaac says that he and Roman find Coco annoying, although they play together constantly. I ask why.

Isaac: Everything we make, she destroys.
Me: She'll work for the Arts Council one day.

[Tumbleweed]

Isaac informs me: 'The worst way to die is boiled. The best way is a heart attack in your sleep because then you don't know.'

Isaac returns from a weekend with four school chums including overnight stays. I asked about his 'dummy' which we refer to, in code, as 'duh.' He said he'd managed to sneak it into his mouth, undetected.

Me: Imagine if they'd seen! Imagine if those boys had seen 'duh.'
Isaac: I'd be ruuuuined!

I laugh. He mimes typing and says, 'Is that going in the ...?'

Oct 13th School gate I'm in a black leather jacket from a junk shop. He hates it. 'I do not like that jacket. It looks like you're going to ride a motorbike or something .... it looks really 80s.'

Oct 14th I dropped him at school in the morning. Usually Celia's job. As we approached the gate, hand in hand, he gave me a crash-course in how to behave. 'Call me Isaac,' he said quietly. He feared I might use a baby name – Toots, Button or Monster – that would attract derision from his classmates. I mustn't hug him either. 'Just *Goodbye Isaac*,' he said.

'OK,' I agreed. '*Goodbye Isaac*. And I'll give you a little squeeze, like this. Ready?' I squeezed his hand. 'I like that,' he said. I squeezed it again as we reached the gate.

'Have a good day,' I said. 'And *Goodbye* ***Buster***.'

He glared in mock outrage. I'd broken my promise but I'd called him 'Buster' – a laddish title that would cause him no difficulty.

Oct 27th **(Age 8 years, 4 months)** I said, 'Mummy's sulking today. She's very good at it.' Isaac: 'Could she go on *Britain's Got Talent*?'

Of a school friend's command of German.

Isaac: He knows fluent.

Nov 1st He tells me Celia often compliments other parents on their children's names. Isaac: 'If she thinks they're good names why didn't she give them to me?'

Nov 10th Isaac on penology. 'I think if you kill someone you should be killed.' I mention the difficulty over female killers like Ruth Ellis. I remind him of the Magdala, where she shot her lover dead, with bullet holes visible which he remembered. 'Do they still have the gun marks?' [bullet holes]

Nov 15th We discuss time travel which his magazine predicts will arrive in 2100 AD – although it's unclear why they haven't popped back to tell us. He says 'I can tell the future. I'm going to touch that newspaper in two seconds. There. Done. Does that count?'

After playing roulette, in which we broke the bank, he says 'that was a very intense game.'

Celia asks him to tidy away the roulette table. Isaac: 'I'm polishing my Match Attacks.'

Nov 27th (Aged 8 yrs, 5 months) A red-hot coal rolls out of the fire onto the slate fender. I don't react. He's puzzled and asks about the burning coal and the slate.

Isaac: Is that as hot as lava?
Me: Could be.
Isaac: Really?
Me: But it doesn't go through because the slate is a type of stone.
Isaac: Can lava not melt stone?
Me: I don't know.
Isaac: Can it melt diamond?

Dec 2nd I'm about to pay for his cello lessons even though he never practises. Cost, £195.

Isaac: Not much.
Me: But you never practise. You're supposed to do half an hour a day.
Isaac: 20 minutes!
Me: All right, when did you last do 20 minutes?

Isaac's guilty face brightens gleefully.

Isaac: Do you know what? I can't remember!

I laugh.

Isaac: Why don't you put that on that?

Meaning write his confession that he never practises on the invoice and send it to the teacher. Tempting.

Dec 5th 'Why do wee and poo come out of different places? Why don't they have just soggy poo? I think diarrhea might be when something blocks your willy. So you just have soggy poo.'

Dec 6th Searching for a toy car which allegedly glowed in the dark. We couldn't find it. Isaac: 'I don't think it can have glown.'

Dec 22nd Isaac wondered if beggars aren't necessarily homeless but are dressing up to look 'beggish.'

Dec 23rd (Aged 8 yrs, 6 months) He tells me 'I'm good at making people do things – with my tears.'

Dec 27th Back from Devon by train. He was climbing up the wall in the connecting corridor. 'Do you have to be tall to be a mountaineer?' I said it helps because tall people are nearer the summit. 'Summit?' New word. I said I didn't want him to be a mountaineer. 'Why not?' I told him it scared me.

Isaac: What other jobs do you not want me to do? Daredevil? Is that a job?

I told him the term was 'stunt man' – probably safer than mountaineering. I assumed he wanted a job I disapproved of. Other way round. He hopes I'll support his career choices

Jan 8th 2015 Isaac toiling homeward with the cello on his back. He begs me to carry it for the last two feet to the house. I refuse.

Me: That would set a very dangerous precedent.
Isaac: What's president?
Me: Precedent. ... an example.
He begs and pleads and says he's bursting to go to the loo – and will I carry the cello the last two feet into the house? I refuse again. He gets furious and shouts. 'You're the worst daddy in the world. And I don't care who hears that.'

I walk on.

Isaac: I wish you weren't my father!
Me: Maybe I'm not.
Isaac: I hope that's true. I wish you were dead.
Me: Come on old chap, we're nearly home now.

Back home he rushes into the sitting-room, dumps the cello, grabs a stick from the firewood basket and hits me with it, snapping it in two. Then he hits me with the stump.

Me [parrying his blows]: I thought you were going to the loo. Forgot all about that didn't you?!

An hour later, with a big sigh.

Isaac: All right, Daddy. I forgive you!

Jan 11th He sees the Style section of the *Sunday Times* where Jeremy Clarke's picture by-line once appeared. Isaac thinks the new by-line is Jeremy but it's Cosmo Landesman. I explain that Jeremy's been sacked but it's all right because he's still at the *Spectator*.

Me: He's the best writer at the *Spectator*.

Isaac thrusts an aggressive finger at me.

Isaac: And the second best is you!

Feb 2nd (Aged 8 years, 7 months) He thinks inventions may yield riches. 'Would I get a lot of money if I invented a tennis racket that's also a television?'

Home by tube.

Isaac: Do you believe in God?
Me: Not really.
Isaac: Can a leech kill you?
Me: No.
Isaac: Where are leeches found?
Me: Not sure.
Isaac: Do you even know what a leech is?
Me: Roughly.
Isaac: If you were bitten by a thousand leeches would you die?
Me: Possibly.

Bertie had told him he'd been bitten by a leech. Isaac wanted to know how close to death Bertie had been.

He told me in a whisper that he didn't like living in our street because 'there are Moslems.' I said he already knew plenty of Moslems, like Seskin. But they don't count as they don't alarm him.

Feb 12th After school. He asks me what's my favourite Greek tragedy. I say *Oedipus*.

Isaac: Ortheus?
Me: Orpheus.
Isaac: Ortheus.
Me: It's Orpheus.
Isaac: I thought it was Ortheus.
Me: Orpheus. Anyway Oedipus is different. It's about a man who marries his mother.
Isaac: That is illegal.

Me: It was back then too. He marries his mother. And they have children.
Isaac: Is it a comedy?

He wanted to buy a framed picture of Venice for Celia's birthday. In the evening, lying on the bed, he pointed to the opposite wall where it would hang. (They share a room.) 'And when you wake up' he said 'it's like you've crashed into Venice.'

On the tube, he told me the most intelligent land mammal is an elephant.

Isaac: Do you know what the most intelligent sea creature is?
Me: No.
Isaac: Octopus. And what does it do when it gets bored?
Me: What?
Isaac: Kills itself.

Feb 27th (Aged 8 yrs, 8 months) Leo and Isaac in the park. Leo due to fly to Ireland later.

Me: There's a pub over there, Leo, it's called Top of the Morning.
Isaac: That sounds Irish.
Me: It is Irish. Although they don't actually say it in Ireland.
Isaac: Is it racist?

March 2nd Unanswerable question #187 'Who invented the handle?'

Isaac: Did they have Jay-Two-Oh [fruit juice] when you were little?
Me: No.
Isaac: Toilet paper?

April 19th Isaac recalls the strange questions he used to ask 'when I was little.' He remembered a question I hadn't recorded.

'Who invented the beard?'

He said, ‘when I was little I used to think God had a beard that went all the way down to Africa.’

Then he asked me to tell him who invented the beard. He assumed I would know.

Gap of two years lost!

In June 2017, my computer crashed and I lost reams of Isaac material. Intermittently I recalled some of the vanished sayings which I added as they came to me. The diary proper resumes, below, on June 4, 2017.

***Missing**: (without dates, except where I recall the date)*

Isaac: Did you know that a blue whale has eyes the size of a beach ball?

I played him a David Bowie track for the first time. Isaac, unimpressed. 'I don't think he's very talented.'

As I leave to see *Hamlet*, I tell him it's about a man who kills his uncle. Isaac: Because he didn't buy him an ice cream?

For his 9th birthday Celia bought him a giant panda almost as large as he was. I asked him how it felt to be nine. 'Same as before – just with a panda.'

Nov 30th 2015 (Isaac, aged 9 yrs, 5 months) Tube conversation about Woody Allen on his 80th birthday

Isaac: When Woody Allen dies will it be all over the newspapers?
Me: Yes.
Isaac: When David Cameron dies will it be all over the newspapers?
Me: Yes.
Isaac: When you die will it be all over the newspapers?
Me: No.
Isaac: Why?
Me: I'm not famous.
Isaac: You never know.

I told him about Taki, the writer, who was jailed for smuggling coke through Heathrow. Isaac asked what coke does. I said it makes you happy. Isaac: 'Why? Is it illegal to be happy?'

Celia woke up hungover, bad-tempered. Isaac was annoying her and he accused her of being drunk the previous night. I'd told Isaac that forgetfulness was a side-effect of drunkenness so he quizzed her about the previous night's events until she got a question wrong. Then he renewed his accusations that she was drunk. She shouted. 'Stop it. Go away!' He shouted back. 'You were seven out of ten – and Kitten doesn't like shouting!'

('seven out of ten drunk')

Age **Ten**

Resuming

June 4th 2017 (Isaac 10 years, 11 months)

Isaac: 'Have you ever seen Dr Strange-glove?'

Watching a scary episode of *Dr Who*, Isaac becomes self-parodic. 'I have to face my fear!'

June 9th 2017 Explaining discipline at Hill House International School. 'Three detentions is a suspension and three suspensions is an expell-iation.'

Age Eleven

June 25th 2017 (Aged 11 yrs, 2 days) Talking about famous last words.

Me: Who said 'into thy hands O Lord, I commend my spirit?'
Isaac: Was it the actor who played Father Ted?

July 8th The park. He picked a blackberry that looked ripe but wasn't. He chewed. 'I feel like I'm eating a knife.'

'Technically chess is racist because white moves first, every time. But it was invented in a time of racism.'

Aug 28th 2017 (Aged 11 yrs, 2 months) Isaac brushing his teeth. 'Do you know that every person in the world has as many bacteria as there are people in the world? So I have seven billion bacteria.'

Sept 17th Isaac: Can you get identical cat twins? Like Matty and Ollie.

Sept 30th (Aged 11 yrs, 3 months) Seeing Ozzy Osborne on TV. Isaac: 'He looks like a cross between John Lennon and someone who was born deformed. Oh no, I didn't mean John Lennon, I meant Elton John.'

Isaac's theory of JFK's assassination. The 'assassinator' of Lee Harvey Oswald (Jack Ruby) acted out of revenge because they'd conspired to kill JFK together but Lee Harvey Oswald cheated and shot JFK on his own.

After a philosophy class. Isaac: 'What's that word in Greek for a place where everyone comes and shares ideas?' I said 'agora.' He tells me the school is holding an 'agora' for people to share ideas.

Me: Have you heard of agoraphobia?

Isaac: No.
Isaac: Fear of sharing ideas.

[Joke fails]

Oct 25th (Aged 11 yrs, 4 months) Isaac has no middle name – he's plain Isaac Evans. 'Everyone always says, Oh my God, you haven't got a middle name, and I say ... nor has James Bond.'

He wants 'Danger' as his middle name. Yet he's amused to learn that, aged six, he wanted the middle name 'Soldier.'

Nov 17th The park. Talking about Alexander the Great.

Me: He conquered the world.
Isaac: The whole world?!
Me: The known world.
Isaac: Ah! There's a catch!

Watching David Attenborough discussing oceans on TV. Isaac: 'The world is basically a pond with lilies floating on it. And we're the frogs. Seven billion of us.'

We watch a whale suckling a calf.

Isaac: I know. Whale cheese! Do you know the most expensive cheese in the world?
Me: Whale cheese?
Isaac: Donkey cheese. Because there's something in cow's milk that makes it turn into cheese but it's not in donkey's milk but there's one man who knows how to do it.

I laughed, and I asked if he minded. He didn't mind but he wasn't curious about my laughter. I asked if he found it odd that only one man in the whole world made donkey cheese. He didn't find it odd. Just shrugged and said 'it's in Alaska.'

Nov 19th 2017 Isaac said he'd learned about Newton and his three laws. I asked what they were. He said 'one, two and three,' as if that were the answer I sought.

Isaac on 'recently' and its usages. 'When I say recently it's two weeks ago. When adults say recently it's three years.' He accused me of saying recently to mean ten years ago.

Nov 22nd Budget day. I explained that it's the government's yearly spending plan. I asked him to guess how much.

Isaac: Two billion pounds?
Me: About 800 billion.
Isaac: 800 billion! How many drones is that!

'Drone' is Isaac for £1,000. He calculates values using this rate of exchange.

Tube. Isaac plays a game of world microbial destruction on his phone. Soon he's killed 247 people. Five minutes later: 'I've killed more people than small-pox' – [over a billion]. By the end of the journey he's killed everyone on earth.

Dec 9th 2017 (Aged 11 yrs, 5 months) Talking about Tiny Tim in Dickens, I mentioned that he was 'crippled.' A new word to Isaac. 'It's a really horrible word.'

Dec 14th I bought a biography of Voltaire.

Isaac: Was he French?
Me: Oui.
Isaac: 'Oui' ... ? As in 'We Are Family?'

Dec 15th Discussion about whether mankind will ever live on another planet and which planets, apart from Mars, have received space probes. I said Mars was the only habitable planet and that Jupiter is covered in smog.

Isaac: On Jupiter it rains diamonds.
Me: I like that idea. Raining diamonds.
Isaac: It's not an idea. It's a fact.

Getting the Christmas tree. Much arguing about its size. Isaac says 'the bigger the better. Mind you not everything's the bigger the better like a brain tumour.'

Jan 1st 2018 (Aged 11 yrs, 6 months) He asks me what's the worst film I've ever seen.

Me: I don't know.
Isaac: What's the 45th worst film you've ever seen?
Me: .... Uh?
Isaac: What's the 320th worst film you've ever seen?

Jan 26th (Aged 11 yrs, 7 months) Returning from school, we're discussing if McDonalds is bad for you. I said it was fine. Isaac said it was stuffed with sugar. We discussed how many calories a cheeseburger contains.

Isaac: One thousand.
Me: No!
Isaac: Yes.
Me: How many calories do you need a day?
Isaac: Six thousand.
Me: No.
Isaac: No. That's in the Antarctic.

Jan 28th He tells me space is more polluted than China.

Me: Where did you learn that?
Isaac: In my book of facts. Do you believe it?
Me: If it's a fact it doesn't matter if I believe it or not.

Feb 3rd Watching *Sherlock* I noticed that Sherlock stole evidence from crime scenes.

Isaac: Is that illegal?
Me: Yes.
Isaac: If you solve a crime and you're not the police do you go to jail?

Later in the episode, a celebrity fitness instructor was killed and Sherlock inspected her body in a mortuary. Isaac: 'If you see a celebrity and it's dead does that count as meeting them?'

[Unclear why he said 'it's dead' rather than 'they're dead.' He was pondering a visit to Michael Jackson's grave and thought it might 'count' as meeting him]

Feb 8th Isaac's school project with the CIA – namely Charif, Isaac and Andreas – is about global warming. Isaac's speech ends:

'Also, always remember. STOP GLOBAL WARMING, NOT EVERYONE CAN SWIM.'

Feb 10th Isaac returns after having lunch with elderly friends of Celia in Canterbury. 'Do you want to hear a major design flaw with the German first world war helmet?'

The flaw was the spike. British soldiers used it for target practice. If a bullet hit the spike the helmet would be snapped backwards, held firm by the under-chin strap, breaking the wearer's neck.

Feb 17th Eve of Celia's birthday. Isaac muses out loud about making her breakfast in bed. He remembers she doesn't like food in bed. He considers making her a cup of tea but thinks he'll oversleep. 'I could tell her I was *going* to make it.' He thinks this will add to her birthday joy.

Later, he's perched on the sofa. He tells me:

'I'm watching a video, *Eight Kids Who Out-smarted their Kidnappers.*'

He has a 'McDonalds Club' with Max and Edward but they both owe him money for McDonalds. So the club has lapsed. He said Max owes him £8.

'Max is waiting till his tooth falls out to pay me because he gets £10 for that.'

I said Isaac should knock his tooth out for him. Isaac had already offered to do it.

Feb 23rd (Aged 11 yrs, 8 months) Celia went to see *Les Noces* by Stravinsky. We listened to a YouTube version. Ghastly tuneless shrieking. I told Isaac that Stravinsky was usually quite good. He gave his verdict on *Les Noces*: 'I think he wrote it when he was drunk. Or bored. And threw it away and the cleaner found it in the bin.'

March 4th Isaac spends an hour making three trays of macaroons. We put them in the oven. They burn. Isaac's disappointment lasts two seconds. 'That was a fail. Good luck with the washing up.'

March 22nd Watching *Rear Window.* Enter Grace Kelly. I ask if she's pretty.

Isaac: She looks like that other one. They all look the same.
Me: Marilyn Monroe?
Isaac: Blonde hair, red lips. ... All she needs is a beauty spot.

He says women in 1950s films 'look like Hitler wanted everyone to look, white, blonde, blue eyes.' I said that included him, with blonde hair and blue eyes.

'My eyes are grey,' he said. [In fact, blue]

March 25th 2017 (Aged 11 years, 9 months) He told me Oprah was standing in the US election.

Isaac: Can anyone be president?
Me: Anyone born in America.
Isaac: Why don't thousands of people do it?
Me: It's expensive.
Isaac: Oh, do you have to pay?

April 25th (Aged 11 yrs, 10 months) Isaac researching domestic calamities on the internet, asks me 'how do you put out a grease fire?' I suggest a blanket. He's disappointed I didn't get it wrong.

Isaac: Would you try water?
Me: No.
Isaac: That's the worst thing to put on a grease fire.

He's annoyed to learn that his friend Edward is going to be Sir Edward when he inherits his father's baronetcy. On the upside, everyone calls Edward 'Orang Utan.'

Isaac invents a card game, *Gone Wild*, about animals becoming extinct. I advise him to find a distributor for the game. He fears the distributor will take some of the money.

Me: They'd take a bit. Quite a lot probably.
Isaac: Let's hope it's not most.

Isaac complaining about an unpopular boy, Misha, whose company will be inflicted on Isaac & Roman at a theme park in Windsor. To show us how annoying Misha is, Isaac walks into the sitting room and says 'wait...'

He walks backwards slowly around the room like a robot, saying 'he's really really really really really really REALLY' ... [he sits, and finishes] 'ANNOYING!'

Celia disparages this attitude. 'Isaac you are being taken – at huge expense – to the largest Aqua Park in the world.'
Isaac: 'No. The largest is in Germany.'

Me and Isaac watching *Jobs* about Steve Jobs. He's a cold, arrogant, pedantic loner. Like me. Isaac says it first.

Isaac: He's like you.
Me: Yeah, he is.
Isaac: But you're not such a good entrepreneur* and you're not as good with computers.

[* pronounced 'untrue-pru-newer']

June 15th 2018 (Aged 11 yrs, 11 months) Discussing David Cameron.

Isaac: What's he doing?
Me: Nothing. He's not even an MP.
Isaac: He resigned?
Me: But he still has bodyguards, 24 hours a day.
Isaac: Because people hate him so much? Because he resigned?

Age Twelve

June 29th 2018 Constant lobbying. He wants us to buy him a drone or a chameleon – or both.

His school trip to Mount Snowdon ended in *failure* to summit Snowdon even though a bus takes tourists to the peak by road. The trip cost £500. Isaac awarded it '8 out of 10' – a low score.

Isaac: It wasn't worth 500 pounds. It was worth 200.
Me: Then you owe me 300 pounds.
Isaac: You owe me a drone.

July 8th He asks which country is best at rugby.

Me: New Zealand.
Isaac: England invents all of these games and then is rubbish at all of them.

Aug 14th (Aged 12 yrs, 1 month) Isaac is in Siponto, Italy, with Roman, Coco and River. Over the phone, I ask him if he saw last night's meteor shower.

Isaac: I saw eight which was more than anyone else.
Me: Did Mummy see any?
Isaac: She saw one.
Me: What about Coco? Girls can't see them can they.
Isaac: She saw one.
Me: What about River?
Isaac: He saw two.

[Clearly made up. Then, over the phone I hear:]

Isaac: Stop attacking me, River!

[Ends call – River scratching him]

I sent him long texts and got very short replies. I said he was being monosyllabic explaining that it means 'using one syllable.' Reply: 'Shdn't it have one syllable not 5?'

In Wales, by Tal-y-Llyn, walking around the lake we pass a tiny brook. We discuss how cold it might be and Isaac puts in his hand. 'Same temperature as the Danube,' he says, having just returned from a holiday near the Danube. I pass this to Arfon and Celia. 'Danube temperature.' They laugh. Isaac doesn't see what's funny.

Aug 26th (Aged 12 yrs, 2 months) Isaac: 'To kill you, you'd have to smoke 642 kg of weed in 15 minutes.' He's started to grade his friends according to how much weed they'll smoke in adulthood. 'I don't think Algy will smoke that much. Billy will.'

Sept 7th Our walk. I asked if he thought God had human characteristics. He talked about Jesus and suggested that God had lots of children whom he dispatched to various planetary bodies, including the Sun, to see how they got on. Jesus got the Earth mission. 'Maybe God doesn't care about humans. It's just a test for his children.'

Sept 18th Isaac phones a friend to ask about homework graded by the teacher. Isaac got 3 out of 11. Isaac: 'You got two and a half out of eleven? I got half more than you.'

Sept 22nd He visits a medical exhibition where an ultrasound is taken of his neck. 'They showed my jiggler.' [Jugular]

Sept 23rd (Aged 12 yrs, 3 months) He asks me a question to which he knows the answer.

Isaac: What's the most famous word Shakespeare invented?
Me: Excellent.
Isaac. And 'break a leg' and 'door-knob.'

I disputed these Shakespearean coinages. I was told I was wrong.

Oct 2nd Discussing the new female Dr Who and sexism. Isaac: 'Imagine if they called her Nurse Who!'

Nov 14th (Aged 12 yrs, 4 months) Talking about a forthcoming European Army. I'm not keen.

Me: Would you die for this country?
Isaac: No! [Pause] Wait. To save everyone in this country? If it was all up to me. Maybe.
Me: Would you die for Europe?
Isaac: If it was all up to me. Maybe.

Nov 18th River, a toddler, took a couple of Isaac's toy cars home with him. I told Isaac and I expected him to be touched and charmed. He felt angry and threatened and ordered me to buy replacement cars, one of which he said had cost '£30' – (false.)

Nov 30th (Aged 12 yrs, 5 months) I found a folded up piece of paper in Isaac's pocket. It was half an inch long, like a flattened cartridge, with a longer thin piece of paper which could be inserted into the cartridge. Along the cartridge the word BOMB was written. He demonstrated it. You insert the long thin piece which primes the fuse. 'It's a nuclear bomb.' He pointed to the nuclear symbol drawn on the fuse which I hadn't noticed. He pulled out the fuse and mimed an explosion with his hands: the fists opposed, then the fingers rapidly loosening and expanding, while vocalising 'BOOM' softly. It all seemed completely real to him.

Dec 2nd A cactus shop. Isaac spots a model flamingo. 'Did you know there are more fake flamingos in the world than real flamingos ... although I'm not sure how they monitor that.'

Dec 3rd Watching *The Apprentice.* I said Alan Sugar was probably born in the same hospital as Isaac. 'You told me that before,' he said. 'And you know what I said?'

Me: What -
Isaac: Same bed?

Dec 7th River, 3, comes into my room with Coco. 'Where's der dat?' says River. (Coco translates: 'Where's the cat?') I said, 'the cat's called Kitten.' 'Ditten, Ditten,' calls River and he runs around the house calling 'Ditten! Ditten!'

Dec 8th Isaac wants to go out but I have to fetch his clothes for him, which I do. He rejects my choices. 'Daddy. You can take those all back upstairs because they're all wrong.' Later he asks me to get him a chocolate biscuit and Turkish delight (two pieces.) And after some argument I comply. I hand him the Turkish delight.

Isaac: Actually, the service here is not that good. I'd like to have a word with the manager.

Dec 13th He asks what happens to the probes we send to Mars.

Me: They get left there.
Isaac: We're already littering other planets?

Isaac downstairs. He has some fudge, which he relishes, having received it from school. It's kept in the fridge. I give him three pieces and he hands me one back to eat. Very generous. I go upstairs. Five minutes later. 'Daddy? Can I have some more fudge?' I go downstairs and fetch him the fudge from the fridge.

Me: I'm going to have some too.
Isaac: Give me all of it and I'll give you how much you're allowed.

Jan 2nd (Aged 12 yrs, 6 months) Isaac notices I haven't drunk since Christmas Day. But he says that abstinence doesn't affect my mood.

Me: So why did you keep asking me to stop drinking?
Isaac: [German accent] Because ve did not know ze vays of ze Lloyd.

He spends 10 hours making a huge Saturn V out of Lego & it's finally complete. (Cost, £109.)

Me: Where shall we put it?
Isaac: I was thinking on the edge of my desk. Or do you think we should keep it where more people can see it?

Jan 5th Isaac, angry for some reason, keeps calling me Hitler. Says that my similarities to Hitler have convinced him that re-incarnation is true. Later he apologises for calling me Hitler. Later still, he gets angry again and thinks up a new insult. But he's unsure how I'll react so he previews it with 'it's very, very rude.' I tell him to throw it at me. He refers to a miscarriage my mum had when I was two, in 1965, which he knows about.

Isaac: That abortion your mum had. I wish that was you.

I found this hilarious. He kept up the attacks. He hit me on the head and demanded that I buy Celia something very costly and pointless, e.g. a garden re-landscaping project. I refused. He said he was going to kill me as soon as he reached my height. He asked about the details, the age of legal responsibility & his likely term of imprisonment. I thought he was really planning it. I was upstairs working. He said he was going to get a knife.

(Later, he was worried I might tell my sister and brother about the abortion gag.)

He went down to fetch the threatened knife. Much noisy rummaging in cutlery drawers. Up he came. I was apprehensive. Outside my room he said he needed something sharper. Back downstairs. More noisy rummaging in cutlery drawers. Back up he came. He charged into my room brandishing a spoon. Which he found hilarious.

Jan 8th Isaac writes to the Queen on a tiny oblong scrap of paper, one inch by two inches, with a first class stamp.

Dear The Queen,

My name is Isaac. Nice to see you. Well, I didn't see you but anyway. I don't know if you remember but my Mum gave you flowers at King's Canterbury School about 38 yrs ago.

From Isaac

PS Sorry it's so small

Addressed to 'Buckingham Palace, London, England, Europe, Earth.'

I spend a day looking after River. He seeks out toys and when he finds one that he likes he says 'no way!' or 'I knew it!' or 'I know it!' I was relaxing on an armchair with him on the sofa. He took a cushion.

River: I'm going to hit your head with a cushion.
Me: I'd rather you didn't. But go on then. [He's only three]

He climbed down with the cushion in his hand and put it under my head, as a headrest. So 'hit' was his best guess for 'support.'

Jan 20th Celia left pancake mix in the kitchen. Isaac, on the sofa watching YouTube, gave me orders. 'Two biscuits.' He meant chocolate biscuits.

Me: Do you want a pancake?
Isaac: [showing two fingers] Two.

[meaning two chocolate biscuits and dismissing the pancake offer]

Me: I'll make you a pancake if you like?
Isaac: Why are you interrogating me?

(which is what I always ask him.)

I make him the pancake, according to his instructions, with Nutella and chopped banana. I serve it to him on a tray. He pokes it with a fork. 'It's oily!' This infuriated me as I'd spent ages making it. I told him to eat it and show some gratitude. 'I need a knife.' I brought him a knife. 'Not that type. A butter knife.' Alas I brought him that as well.

After Celia had a massive hangover we discussed it.

Me: She's still drunk of course.
Isaac: No, she's got a hangover it's not the same as being drunk.
Me: It is.
Isaac: It's not.
Me: Isaac, I think I know more about hangovers than you.
Isaac: We did it in chemistry!

When Auntie Sheila died, Feb 21st, he was away in Porthcawl and I phoned him. He said, 'did you hear what happened to your aunt?' Odd phrasing.

March 1st 2019 (Aged 12 yrs 8 months) Isaac was given a beautiful pair of old brown leather shoes by Roman. Isaac not tempted. 'They look like elves' shoes. Can we sell them?'

March 2nd Discussions with Celia and Thomas about costly garden refurbishments which Isaac has strong ideas about. My contribution? Paying for it.

Me: Isaac, how much influence do you think you have over this project?
Isaac: Quite a lot.
Me: How much influence do you think I have?
Isaac: Zero.

Isaac tells me about twins, a year below him, aged 11. The mother is 60 and runs a shipping firm. (She's Greek – so probably a family concern). The father is 68. 'What does he do?' Isaac knew I'd find this funny: 'He's an aspiring writer.' He said that the father had never had a job.

Their house in South Kensington is three homes knocked together with a garden 'as large as a basketball pitch. ... in *South Kensington!'* he says scandalised. He understands the financial realities of this and he quoted the value of the property. 'Forty million pounds.' And they have a bolthole in the Caribbean which they rent out. 'It's $170,000 a week. Minimum two weeks.' I like the 'minimum two weeks.' Isaac told me Justin Bieber stayed there. 'I hope he cleared up after him.'

Isaac has a philosophy teacher! I explained to Isaac that free will, being an illusion, compels us to believe in free will rather than in predestination. So our belief in free will is predestined. He wasn't interested. 'My philosophy teacher's favourite film is *Die Hard*.' I said, 'oh God. That's completely destroyed my faith in him as a philosophy teacher.'

[Isaac didn't get this]

Isaac: He also likes *Minority Report.*

March 30th (Aged 12 yrs, 9 months) He told me Jesus wasn't born at Christmas.

Me: I know, he falsified his date of birth so he could claim unemployment benefit.
Isaac: Really!

April 8th Isaac about to go to the Azores with Celia who suffers an explosive fit of pre-holiday rage. Isaac retreats to the kitchen & won't be budged. 'I'm not going on holiday with a mad woman,' he says evenly.

I phoned him in the Azores. He was disappointed that a whale-spotting trip had been called off because of low cloud. 'The whales were cancelled.'

May 29th (Aged 12 yrs, 11 months) Half term. Isaac bored. He refused to go to Leo's because his trousers were wet and the spare pair had a split which he couldn't mend because the sewing-kit had no needle. All fictional excuses. (He's nearly 13). To amuse himself he tormented me, sat in my room, turned off my music, complained of boredom. I left for the library, with my laptop, which slightly upset him. I said I'd be back soon. Meanwhile his barely-even-damp trousers dried on the line. As soon as I left him alone, he started texting me I the library.

'Help!!'

Then -

'Help.'

Then -

'I am going to go now because I'm going to Leo's or I'm being kidnapped.'

Then -

'I found trousers.'

I came back and took him to Leo's. He was wearing a dry pair of trousers that he'd known about all along. I told him that his texts crying for 'help' failed because a kidnapper wouldn't let a hostage send texts. He said he hoped I'd fear someone was breaking into the house.

Age Thirteen

Nov 6th 2019 Isaac listening to *Free Bird* by Lynyrd Skynyrd. 'Seventies music,' I said and I asked if music then was better than now. Isaac: 'Yes. But it depends on the genre.'

Then, about Lynyrd Skynyrd.

Isaac: They're really racist and homophobic.
Me: They're from Alabama.
Isaac: And probably really inbred as well.
Me: That's bigoted. Or is that a joke?
Isaac: Joke.

Nov 10th Going to Leo's. Isaac: 'When Brexit's over there's going to be Brexit 2, leaving the UN, then Brexit 3, leaving NATO, then Britain will break away from the earth.' Outside Leo's house he asks, 'will there ever be another Crusade?'

Nov 13th Isaac went to *The Marriage of Figaro* the previous night and woke up late so Celia emailed the school claiming he had a migraine. He told me he was going to do homework all day. After seven hours of YouTube, he was still on the sofa.

Me: How's the homework?
Isaac: Good. Very good.

I went to the shop & got him mince pies with iced tops. Isaac: 'I'm not a big fan of mince pies. Just one. I'll have one now. Take the rest away.'

I got him an Actimel yogurt from the fridge. He drank it, put the empty container on the stool and said 'done.'

December 9th Isaac asked what verb is derived from 'fraud.'

Me: Defraud.
Isaac: Defraud. Sounds like the opposite, 'to defraud an account', like you're making it honest.

Isaac's advent calendar, stuffed with chocolate, arrived but the package was delivered to our neighbour. Isaac didn't want to fetch the package. He felt it was a job for his parents. Celia returned home having become a Catholic the previous day. As it was the Feast of the Annunciation – a holyday of obligation – I asked if she'd been to Mass. 'I've had a very long day!' she said. Skipped Mass, clearly. She started her angry supper performance in the kitchen. Isaac was pestering me to collect the chocolate advent calendar. I hate collecting parcels from neighbours.

Me: You get it, Isaac. It's next door.
Isaac: I've only got my shirt on. I haven't got my shoes on. Will you get it?
Me: Why can't you?
Isaac: I can't.
Me: OK.
Isaac: In five minutes?
Me: No.

I rejected his deadlines.

Isaac: Twenty minutes?
Me: No.

He said he wanted his scarf back in that case – the scarf he gave me for Christmas.

Me: You shouldn't attach conditions to gifts.

I gave him the scarf back. He asked for some juice. I went into the kitchen where Celia was cooking.

Me: Isaac's pestering me to get his advent calendar.
Celia: Oh, I'll get it.

I went back to Isaac, in triumph.

Me: Mummy says she'll get your calendar.

Isaac saw the danger here – Celia is much harder to coerce than me. And he didn't dare hassle her directly. He entered the kitchen, tentatively.

Isaac: Mummy? Daddy said you're getting the advent calendar.
Celia: I'm cooking your supper!

His aim was to get Celia to withdraw her promise to collect the calendar. Then the responsibility would revert to me. He set to work. But Celia assumed that any request from Isaac would involve extra hassle for her.

Isaac: Mummy? Just say you're NOT going to get the advent calendar.
Celia: Leave me alone!
Isaac: Say it. Say you're NOT getting it.
Celia: Don't tell me what to do.
Isaac: But just say you're NOT going to get it.
Celia: I'm not your slave. I am cooking your supper, Isaac.
Isaac: Just say it.
Celia: Don't talk to me like that.

A fresh ploy.

Isaac: Who's going to get the advent calendar?
Celia: I don't know. I don't care.
Isaac: Just say you AREN'T.
Celia: No. I'm not going to get it. I'm cooking. And don't tell me what to do!

So he returned to me in triumph and announced that Celia wouldn't get it. And the responsibility was now mine. I wriggled out of it and Celia, after much complaint, collected the calendar. But she didn't go to Mass and became a lapsed Catholic on Day One of her life as a convert. I told Isaac this meant she'd go to hell. He wasn't concerned.

Jan 11th 2020 (age 13 yrs, 6 months) I take Isaac to cover a *Stop the War* rally in London. Isaac mentions Julian Assange. 'I like him. He's like a rebel. He just doesn't care.' Coming home, he asks if I know anyone who was killed in the Blitz.

Me: Of course not.
Isaac: Because our family wasn't here.
Me: Right.
Isaac: Was the Blitz anywhere else? Or was it just London? What about Brighton?
Me: Lots of places, Coventry and Exeter.
Isaac: They got as far as Exeter?
Me: Just once. You know the modern pedestrian shopping mall. That got bombed. It would have been lots of lovely 18th century houses before.
Isaac: Oh. ... But then again, there'd have been no Build-A-Bear. [A bear shop, where he got Choobacca]. So thank you Germany – for Choobacca.

Isaac likes Dennis Skinner because he makes jokes at the state opening of Parliament.

Feb 15th Isaac: 'An elephant is the only mammal that can't jump.'

Feb 29th 2020 Baby Wilf born to Boris. He asks if I'm pleased that Boris has a new baby.

Me: Yes.
Isaac: Which number?

Me: Six.
Isaac: Sixty what?

April 7th 2020 He announced that I 'owe him' four pounds. I said I'd pay him later.

Isaac: It doubles every day
Me: No, it doesn't.
Isaac: Now it doubles every five hours. So you owe me four pounds, then eight, and 16, and 32 and slowly it'll turn into a drone.

[Drone – £1,000]

April 11th He asks me where *Apocalypse Now* was filmed. Vietnam, he suggests. I tell him Vietnam was a communist dictatorship in the 1970s – bad for filming. It was filmed in the Philippines. He says he'd like to visit the Philippines. I said: 'or you could hire a cleaner – and the Philippines could come to you.' He said that was 'funny but racist.'

He often asks which countries I could and couldn't visit during my gap year in 1981/1982. He's surprised that the no-go zones include Vietnam and Cambodia but not Thailand, Malaysia, Indonesia or China. He wondered if Japan was off-limits. I tell him Japan was a democracy.

April 19th He read *Dulce Et Decorum Est* by Wilfred Owen and I quoted the parts I liked. Isaac enjoys the goriness of it. I told him Owen was killed in the final week of the first world war and that WB Yeats hated Owen. 'Nothing but blood, dirt and sucked sugar stick,' said Yeats of Owen, 'not worthy of Poet's Corner in a country newspaper.'

Isaac asked when Yeats had died. 'September 1st 1939.' Then I realised this was the day that Hitler invaded Poland. 'In effect he died on the first day of the second world war,' I said. So Isaac imitated Yeats, 'oh God, not another Wilfred Owen!' He mimed Yeats slashing Owen's throat many times.

The park. I pointed out that some couples have a dog instead of a baby. Now he describes any childless couple with a dog as 'a dog instead of a baby people.' He applies this to Celia's friends, e.g. Emma Christmas who has a furniture shop, many dogs and no kids.

'Is she a dog instead of a baby person?'

May 23rd Isaac knows all about Hiroshima. There were two bombs, Big Boy and Little Boy. The Hiroshima bomb used just one per cent of its uranium and was therefore intended to be 100 x more destructive than it was (according to Isaac.) The mission was changed at the last minute because the intended target, a northern city whose name he couldn't recall, was covered by cloud. He likes to quote the statement of surrender by the Japanese emperor. 'The enemy has overwhelmed us with their cruel bombs.'

He loves chameleons. Celia went to a mums' party and was keen for Isaac to come too. She offered to buy him a chameleon if he agreed. I thought of a punchline for a gag 'stand-up chameleon.' So we imagined a set-up. I suggested, 'what do you call a funny lizard?' Isaac suggested a different set-up. 'What's the funniest reptile?' I preferred his. Shorter. But 'funny lizard' is itself funny.

Age **Fourteen**

Sept 5th 2020 Celia has a day out with Olga, having spent all of yesterday afternoon at the hair-dressers followed by supper with Angel & Thomas. I ask if Isaac thinks Celia might be 'nattered out.' He says, 'Mummy never gets nattered out. If they ever finally invent perpetual motion they'll find Mummy's nattering somehow being used as the power source.'

Sept 6th Isaac bored at 2 pm on Sunday afternoon after a trip to Mrs Miggins had been cancelled.

Isaac: Alexa? How many days are there in a million years?

Sept 8th We discussed Max's Russian parents, Vlad and Katya, and their possible income sources. Isaac imagined Katya running a pop-up stall near the American embassy selling tea (with polonium) and owning a flat adjoining the embassy and drilling very quietly with a hand-drill which she turns once every 6 hours. Isaac looked Vlad up on LinkedIn and found he worked for Guinness, then for a Russian vodka company.

'VODKA,' said Isaac.

As an acronym we decided it stands for 'Vlad's Obviously Dodgy Killing Association.' Isaac likes imagining violence. He asked me how many people were killed in the Great Storm of 1987. I said 'one, by a falling branch.' He enacted the death with sound effects. He often passes the Iranian embassy in Knightsbridge and he imagines that the 1980 siege is still underway. All talk of violence is punctuated with mime. He sprays machine-gun fire and does the noise by trilling with his tongue. He talks about fighting his way out of sieges or armed robberies.

Oct 3rd Isaac told me about his love of trivia – 'my facts.' Some people like his 'facts' and ask for more. Some people resent them. James, very competitive, dislikes his facts but Niko welcomes them.

He's started a restaurant club. They sample a new restaurant every week and review it (so far only verbally). Lad's growing up.

Oct 10th 2020 I was watching Isaac and Oscar's short film. In the film Isaac is caught by a Monster and gets dragged into the forest. Cut to a close-up of Isaac suffering horrific torments.

Me: Oh my God! What's he doing to you!?
Isaac [off-hand]: Eating me.

Oct 18th Isaac asked me if a woman got sick when she had an abortion. I said I was the wrong person to ask. I mentioned his scan at 13 weeks and he enacted a violent abortion involving a knife and sound effects. I said, 'Isaac? That's your own abortion you're talking about.' He thought this was funny and imagined me and Celia examining his 13-week scan and commenting: 'He looks really annoying. Look, nah, I don't think so. Can we get rid of this one and start again?'

Then we went into a shop –

Isaac: Someone said they used to do it with a coat-hanger but I don't believe that.
Me: Yeah. They did. Abortions in hospitals were illegal. So it was do-it-yourself.

This surprised him. In the shop we got stuck behind a sluggish old dear who wanted lottery tickets and Dettol. She was fussy. Not this Dettol, that Dettol. Not that Dettol, this Dettol – which had to be fetched from the back by a brain-dead cashier. I was fuming as the old dear kept asking for this Dettol or that Dettol. Eventually she chose no Dettol! During this interminable delay I ground my teeth in fury and Isaac said, under his breath, 'calm, Daddy, calm.' Outside the shop I cruelly impersonated the near-dead old dear. Isaac was outraged. 'Daddy! That's so mean.' But the impersonation purged my anger.

Me: Hitler was like that. *A man kept waiting is a man brought to heel.* He hated being kept waiting.
Isaac: Another thing you've got in common with him.

Jan 4th 2021 (age 14 yrs, 6 months) Isaac and I have an argument about Covid masks and I tell him he'll still be wearing a mask in 50 years' time, and defaulters will be imprisoned. I cite the example of pub closing hours that were imposed during the Great War but not lifted till the 1990s. He checks on the government website which incorrectly tells him the rules changed in 1988. I tell him this is false. He says 'you are so desperate to prove me wrong.'

Me: No, I'm just offering you the correct information.

This infuriates him. In revenge, he pronounces 'aitch' with an 'h' which he knows I hate. 'Haitch!' He walks into the kitchen as I'm washing up. 'Haitch,' he says, 'haitch, haitch, haitch, haitch, haitch!'

April 2021 He tells me I'm an alcoholic. I say that I'm not because I still function whereas a real alcoholic can't do anything. He christens my evening beer 'functioning syrup.'

July 8th 2021 Isaac has to read one book for school this summer. Options –

Franz Kafka, *Metamorphosis*
Ernest Hemingway, *The Old Man and The Sea*
Yann Martell, *Life of Pi*
Mary Shelley, *Frankenstein*

I tell him *Metamorphosis* is the shortest and he looks it up. 10,000 words. He calculates how many words he must read per day to finish it in seven weeks. He has no interest in books. But he loves bookshops, he tells me. He loves the idea of reading. He just hates *reading.* He fails to read a single page of any of the four books over the summer.

Age Fifteen

November 13th 2021 I offer him a chocolate Hobnob but I fear he may not recognise the iconic 1980s biscuit.

Me: Do you know Hobnobs?
Isaac: Do I know Hobnobs? That's like asking a Welsh person, 'do you know what a sheep is?'

Feb 20th Isaac programmes Siri to say three things to me. He can activate each of these statements from his phone:

'Daddy, you're being pretentious.'
'Shsh, Daddy. Go to your room.'
'Daddy, can I have a Ginger Snap?'

Feb 25th 2022 Isaac to me, 'you are a rude human.'

Age **Sixteen**

Sept 23rd 2022 Lately, I've begun staging satirical plays.

Isaac: All your plays are tragedies because you think they're comedies.

The End

About the author

Lloyd Evans is a reviewer, parliamentary sketch-writer and playwright. He lives in London. His other books on KDP include *My Year As A Sex Maniac* and *Harry & Meghan – the Play*

He is published by Numisma Books www.numismabooks.co.uk

How My Son Learned to Speak

numismabooks.co.uk

Printed in Dunstable, United Kingdom

78920654R00147